THE BAROQUE LYRIC

MODERN LANGUAGES AND LITERATURE

Literature Editor

J. M. COHEN

The Baroque Lyric

J. M. COHEN

HUTCHINSON UNIVERSITY LIBRARY

LONDON

HUTCHINSON & CO. (*Publishers*) LTD
178–202 Great Portland Street, London, W.1

London Melbourne Sydney
Auckland Bombay Toronto
Johannesburg New York

★

First published 1963

*This book has been set in Baskerville type face. It has
been printed in Great Britain by The Anchor Press,
Ltd., in Tiptree, Essex, on Smooth Wove paper.*

To

HELEN GRANT

Contents

	Introductory note	9
1	The Baroque man and the world in flux	11
2	Desert and charnel-house	30
3	Sacred and profane love	52
4	A stately pleasure-dome	70
5	Gardens and landscapes	89
6	Donne's elephant and Donne's courtier	109
7	The garlands wither	129
8	The dictatorship of the scribes	151
9	The ring of light	177
	Bibliography	201
	Index	205

Introductory note

The English quotations in this book are given in the spelling of the Oxford editions of the poets, or in the case of Marvell of the Muses Library volume (Routledge 1952). Poems in other languages are generally given in modernized forms, except for those of Herrera, which follow his own deliberately idiosyncratic spelling.

Some paragraphs are reproduced, more or less unchanged, from middle-page articles and reviews contributed over the last ten years to *The Times Literary Supplement*. For permission to make fresh use of these judgements I am grateful to the editor and to the proprietors of that journal.

I

The Baroque man and the world in flux

THE TERM Baroque does not yield to exact definition. Its
probable derivation is from the Portuguese word *baroco*,
the term for a misshapen pearl. If a Renaissance work of art
can be thought of as regular and symmetrical, with each
feature balanced and its parts exactly proportioned to one
another and to the whole, its Baroque counterpart will be
irregular and asymmetrical, and its parts will not be so readily
isolated. Thus a typical Renaissance picture will be composed
in receding planes; and a Baroque picture—a Rembrandt
portrait, for example—will draw the eye directly to its central
point, subordinating the rest of the canvas to a single dramatic
effect. Similarly a Renaissance sonnet will state its theme in its
first quatrain, develop it in the next lines, and resolve it in the
final tercet or couplet. The Baroque sonnet, on the other hand,
will state a mood in the opening and go on to intensify without
necessarily resolving it. Alternatively, it may present an image
in its first line and elaborate it without any considerable
increase of emotional tension in the next thirteen.

Between the perfectly rounded pearl, however, and one
that has no symmetry there are countless gradations of form.
The completely spherical and the completely misshapen, at
either end of the line, are comparative rarities. So, in contrasting any pair of lyrical poems, Renaissance and Baroque,
we shall find few that do not possess some features belonging
to both styles. For these styles are much more difficult to distinguish, or to discover in a pure form, than the Classical and
Romantic opposites of the succeeding age. Nor does the
Baroque poem adopt new forms, unused by the Renaissance.

The sonnet and other Italianate measures obtain over the whole Baroque field, and irregular metres are, in general, as rare in the seventeenth century as the sixteenth. Indeed, the majority of the examples, both Renaissance and Baroque, that we shall examine in this book will be sonnets. For not only is the sonnet the most convenient form to examine, since it is short enough to be analysed in its entirety, but it is the medium chosen by the Baroque poets for much of their finest work. Its strict pattern demanded a compression, the absence of which mars many of their lyrics that were written in looser forms, discipline of thought being an elusive virtue in an age when one conceit led easily to the next and stanza melted imperceptibly into stanza. With the exception of the English Metaphysicals, who possessed their own discipline, and the German hymn-writers, whose work was controlled by its liturgical purpose, all the best Baroque poets could be admirably represented in an anthology of sonnets.

Just as the Baroque poet chose no new forms, so he adopted no fresh attitude to his craft or his audience. He saw himself as a cultivated gentleman, for whom poetry was one accomplishment among many; and he was, in fact, by profession a churchman, civil servant, lawyer, or soldier, and a poet only secondarily and at intervals. The audience that he addressed was likewise composed of amateurs, the richest of whom might offer the less exalted his patronage, a secretaryship, or a pension. The professional man of letters was the product of the next century.

The creators of Baroque poetry did not for a moment think of themselves as the founders of a new school, or as in rebellion against the immediate past. The first conscious rebels were for the most part prose-writers, who championed the Moderns against the Ancients in the Battle of the Books, an engagement which did not open until the Baroque age was over. Indeed, the poets whom we shall examine had no common term by which to distinguish those characteristics in their writing that separated them from their immediate fore-runners. Some poets were reproached by their critics for writing in a conceited style, and accusations were made by their enemies that they were over-addicted to Latinisms both verbal and syntactical. But the conceit and the Latinisms were already features of the Renaissance style, and often these critics themselves practised them in their own writing. Certainly most of Luis de Góngora's literary enemies frequently wrote in a manner that we should classify today as Gongoristic.

The term Baroque was thus, of course, unknown in the seventeenth century. Its first recorded use was as a term of denigration employed by art-critics of the Classical epoch. A standard French dictionary of the nineteenth century, which explains Baroque as meaning 'd'une bizarrerie choquante', derives the word not from the Portuguese but from the mnemonic *baroco*, a term used in scholastic argument to denote a particular negative conclusion. Its first recorded use in English is in 1818, and its derivation is given by the *Shorter Oxford Dictionary* as from the Portuguese by way of French. It was not until the end of last century that the German art-critic Heinrich Wölfflin applied it in its modern sense to certain fashions in seventeenth-century sculpture, painting, and architecture, and in the fifty years since he wrote it has been extended, principally by German critics, to cover parallel developments in music and literature. Outside Germany, however, the term is less current, since critics cannot agree, amidst a welter of rival and better-established definitions, which elements in seventeenth-century style can most properly be called Baroque. If the present study succeeds in isolating some of them it will be in no dogmatic sense. The features common to poems by Donne, Góngora, and Marino are probably no more numerous than those in which they radically differ.

The Baroque poem, as has been said, evolves from the Renaissance poem without any sharp break in historical continuity. Many of its chief characteristics were already present in Petrarchism, and indeed in the poetry of Francesco Petrarca himself, whose influence and example prevailed, at least in his native Italy, until the last of Marino's followers had ceased to write. If a date is to be fixed for the style's beginnings one can say that Baroque characteristics became strong in England and Spain during the last decade and a half of the sixteenth century and in France and Italy at about the turn of the century, and that they did not reach Germany and Poland until some twenty-five years later. Halfway through the seventeenth century their hold weakened in England and France, and not long afterwards in Spain, where all culture catastrophically declined in the 1660s. They survived, however, in other countries for a further thirty or forty years, and Marinistic poetry continued to be written in Italy until the beginning of the eighteenth century. It is possible, however, to discover in many poets of an earlier date —the Spaniard Fernando de Herrera (1534–97) and the Portuguese Luis de Camões (1524?–80) are outstanding examples—important elements of a Baroque style, while some outstanding poets of the Baroque age itself—John Milton, for example, and François de Malherbe—wrote not more than one or two poems that display Baroque characteristics.

It is these characteristics that the present book will set out to describe. Several definitions of purely national currency are useful and valid. The Metaphysical and Cavalier schools in England, the Précieux in France, the Marinisti in Italy, and the twin mannerisms of *cultismo* and *conceptismo* in Spain, are universally accepted by critics in their several restricted senses. If some relationship can be discovered, however, that unites them all, transcending frontiers of faith, culture, and language, even though much may still be seen to separate them, something will have been achieved that has not hitherto been attempted in a single study.

A composite portrait of the Baroque style over its whole extent, though perforce impressionistic, may well throw light on each poet by relating him to the rest. Donne can be seen in relation to Andreas Gryphius, a German contemporary who shared some of his preoccupations; and Marvell can be compared to some Spanish poets who, like him, used the ornamental garden as a symbol of peace and reconciliation. In each of my nine chapters, therefore, I shall examine the attitude of the lyrical poets of the age to a particular topic or commonplace in the manner practised by the great German critic Ernst Robert Curtius in his *Europäische Literatur und Lateinisches Mittelalter*[1] and elsewhere, at the same time drawing any parallels that are possible with the attitudes of their contemporaries in other fields of art. Thus I hope to isolate nine principal aspects of the Baroque which, combined, may form a rough poetic portrait of the age.

One outstanding aspect of the Baroque, which is present in almost all the writers whom we shall examine, and particularly in those of the Mediterranean countries, has been defined by the German critic of literature, Fritz Strich, as the 'pictorial' in contrast to the architectural presentation, which he, following Wölfflin's art-criticism, finds predominant in the poetry of the Renaissance.

> The pictorial presentation [he says] shows us the temporal world in its fleeting, changeable and transitory aspects. Time as creator and destroyer, passing and over-throwing, is the primary religious experience of the Baroque. One might equally call it the experience of *vanitas*, of the vanity and transitoriness of the world. What is man? Not, as the Renaissance believed, a sovereign, self-governing, harmonious, cosmic entity, a self-reliant, independent being, but a shadow, a fading music, a passing wave, a reed tossing in the storm and quickly snapped. A dream, a sport, or as one Baroque poet Andreas Gryphius put it, a fantasy of time.[2] This distinguishes the Baroque so signally from the Renaissance, which even in the stream of hurrying time experienced the eternal, self-contained, complete existence, which it represented in its art by lifting it out of the stream of time.[3]

Certainly the seventeenth century had learnt by bitter historical experience that worldly goods and honours were at

---

[1] English translation, Routledge.
[2] 'Ein Irrlicht dieser Zeit'. See sonnet 'Menschliches Elende' in *Deutsche Gedichte des 16 und 17 Jahrhunderts*, ed. Werner Milch.
[3] 'Barockbegriff und Literatur' in *Die Kunstformen des Barockzeitalters*, ed. Rudolf Stamm, pp. 256-7.

best impermanent, and that a man's life counted for little in an era of civil and religious wars. The great nations which had sought to repeat and imitate the grandeur of Rome by spreading their frontiers into other continents had dissolved in internal strife. The Reformation, which had promised a new purity to Christianity, had led to secular warfare and a permanent division between Protestant and Catholic. The Counter-Reformation had saved the Church of Rome, and enabled her to reclaim much of her lost ground, but at the cost of a total suppression of free thought in southern Europe. The optimism of the Renaissance had yielded to a disbelief in the perfectability of man, and a cynical exploitation of his social blindness by a new race of power-politicians, many of whom were churchmen. For the Baroque thinker, poet or religious, life was a flux. What could be observed was no more than an appearance, and in describing these appearances the poet could at best only hint at a reality that he was unable to grasp. If the world was unreal what lay behind it could be described only in a metaphor or symbol, which might not be entirely clear even to the poet himself. 'We must have a private thought', wrote Pascal, 'and even though we speak like the crowd, judge everything by that.'[1] Baroque poetry expresses the 'private thought', while that of the Renaissance speaks of an experience that can be freely conveyed in general terms to other men. Behind all change and appearance, a man has, in the eyes of such a poet as Ronsard, a permanent individuality, and the possibility of a transcendent experience. A clear example of this belief can be found in a typical sonnet (no. XII) of his *Amours* of 1552. The poem is built after the Petrarchan model on a series of contradictions which are resolved in its stoical last line:

> J'espère et crains, je me tais et supplie,
> Or' je suis glace, et ores un feu chaud,
> J'admire tout, et de rien ne me chaut,
> Je me délace, et puis je me relie.

[1] Pensée 311 (Penguin edition).

> Rien ne me plaît si non ce qui m'ennuie,
> Je suis vaillant, et le cœur me défaut,
> J'ai l'espoir bas, j'ai le courage haut,
> Je doute Amour, et si je le défie.
>   Plus je me pique, et plus je suis rétif,
> J'aime être libre, et veux être captif,
> Cent fois je meurs, cent fois je prends naissance.
>   Un Prométhée en passions je suis,
> Et pour aimer perdant toute puissance,
> Ne pouvant rien, je fais ce que je puis.[1]

The powerless lover, racked with contradictions, compares himself to Prometheus, the Titan who suffered martyrdom for bringing the gift of fire to men. Dying and being born a hundred times, Ronsard remains above time. He waits, like Prometheus, to be delivered by Hercules whom he introduces, as the embodiment of his mistress's grace, into the next sonnet, which completes the argument of the first:

> Le plus cruel me serait le plus doux,
>   Si j'espérais, après un long espace,
> Venir vers moi l'Hercule de ta grace,
> Pour délacer le moindre de mes nœuds.[2]

In a similar mood, Ronsard's contemporary Jean du Bellay, in the character of the fearful sailor racked by the storm of his thoughts, pleads for his lady, seen as the goddess and star Venus, to rescue him ('L'Olive', sonnet XLI):

---

[1] I hope and fear, I am silent and beseech. Now I am ice, now a hot fire, I wonder at everything and nothing matters to me, I unloose myself and then tie myself again. Nothing pleases me except what wearies me; I am valiant and my heart fails me; my hopes are low and my courage high; I am afraid of love, and yet I defy it. The more I spur myself the more restless I am. I love to be free and want to be a captive. I die a hundred times and a hundred times am born. I am a martyred Prometheus and, losing all power in order to love, when completely powerless do what I can.

[2] The cruellest [of evils] would be the sweetest to me if I could hope that after a long while the Hercules of your grace would come to me to loosen the least of my bonds.

B

> Le nocher suis, mes pensées sont la mer,
> Soupirs et pleurs sont les vents et l'orage,
> Vous ma Déesse êtes ma claire étoile,
>   Que seule dois, veux, et puis réclamer
> Pour assurer la nef de mon courage,
> Et éclaircir tout ce ténébreux voile.[1]

In these poems of Ronsard and du Bellay there is a consciousness of division and flux. Time, passions, and thought are seen to be passing, yet their passage can be stayed for a moment. Powerful in the acknowledgement of his powerlessness, the poet can summon help from a higher level, and in so doing rise above himself and his own experience. The same ultimate hope of triumph in the midst of loss and disaster is expressed with an even greater force of emotion in the love-sonnets of Luis de Camões, for whom the death of his beloved and the failure of his own powers of love become a supreme opportunity for self-transcendence, and who can accept as a perpetual remembrance that day on which there was 'removed by another will, something which can never be removed' from his own heart:

> Aquela triste e leda madrugada,
> cheia toda de mágoa e de piedade,
> enquanto houver no mundo saudade
> quero que seja sempre celebrada.[2]

If Renaissance man cannot be rescued from the welter of his contradictory moods by the Hercules of his mistress's grace, or even, this side of death, by self-abnegation, at least he perishes heroically. His Baroque successor, on the other hand, casts himself abjectly before God, who alone can save him. Man's human dignity, which had enabled Camões—in the

[1] I am the mariner, my thoughts are the sea, sighs and tears are the winds and the storm, you, my goddess, are my clear star, on whom alone I should, would and can call, to steady the ship of my courage, and light all this darkness that veils me.
[2] That sad and happy dawn, all full of grief and devotion, I would wish to be celebrated for ever, so long as there is sorrow in the world.

sonnets—or his equally unhappy Spanish contemporary Fernando de Herrera—to hymn his cruel mistress's beauty even in the midst of his grief, had yielded to silence or agony:

> Y cuando la razón del mal me afrenta
> en medio del trabajo y pena mía,
> de mi enemiga la belleza canto.[1]

The French poet Jean de Sponde, a Protestant who towards the end of his days made a political conversion to Catholicism, in the last of his sonnets on death confesses to total defeat. Conscious that he cannot of his own strength triumph over the flux of the world, and that his courage must founder, he desperately prays that the wave shall break in vain against the voice and Temple of God within him. The ternary form of Sponde's sonnet contrasts with the purely antithetical construction of Ronsard's 'J'espère et crains'. The two breaks in each line conveying a mood, a constant anxiety, as of a man overwhelmed and sinking:

> Tout s'enfle contre moi, tout m'assaut, tout me tente,
> Et le Monde, et la chair, et l'Ange révolté,
> Dont l'onde, dont l'effort, dont le charme inventé
> Et m'abîme, Seigneur, et m'ébranle, et m'enchante,
>   Quel nef, quel appui, quelle oreille dormante,
> Sans peril, sans tomber, et sans être enchanté,
> Me donras-tu? Ton Temple où vit ta Sainteté,
> Ton invincible main, et ta voix si constante.
>   Et quoi? mon Dieu, je sens combattre maintesfois
> Encore avec ton Temple, et ta main, et ta voix,
> Cet Ange révolté, cette chair, et ce Monde.
>   Mais ton Temple pourtant, ta main, ta voix sera
> La nef, l'appui, l'oreille, où ce charme perdra,
> Où mourra cet effort, où se rompra cette onde.[2]

[1] And when the reason for my disgrace shames me, in the midst of toils and grief I sing my enemy's beauty. (Sonnet, 'Por altos bosques voy'. Oreste Macrí, *Fernando de Herrera*, p. 448.)

[2] Everything swells up against me, everything attacks me, everything tempts me, the world, the flesh and the rebel Angel, whose wave, whose

This same anxiety was already visible in Sponde's hyper-bolical love-poetry. Whilst on the one hand he compared himself to

> . . . . le vaillant Hector, le grand rampart de Troie[1]

and to Carthage and Numantia, cities which resisted the armies of Rome, he also confessed that in his soul a civil war was raging:

> Je sens dedans mon âme une guerre civile:
> D'un parti ma raison, mes sens d'autre parti,
> Dont le brûlant discord ne peut être amorti
> Tant chacun son tranchant l'un contre l'autre affile.[2]

This restless sense of division which pervades Sponde's small body of verse is to be found in an even more pronounced form in the exclamatory and broken sonnets of the German poet Andreas Gryphius, who renounces the whole world and all its illusions, and throws himself on the divine mercy in his sonnet 'An Gott den Heiligen Geist':

> O Weisheit ohne Masz! O reiner Seelen Gast!
> O teurer Gnadenquell! O Trost in herber Last!
> O Regen, der in Angst mit Segen uns befeuchtet!

---

onslaught, and whose deceitful charm overwhelms me, Lord, and racks me, and bewitches me. What ship, what support, what deaf ear will you give me, against danger and falling and enchantment? Your temple in which your Holiness dwells, your invincible hand, and your ever constant voice. But what is this? O God, I very often feel this rebel Angel, this flesh and this world, fighting against your temple, your hand and your voice. Yet your temple, your hand and your voice will be the ship, the support, the ear against which this charm will fail, this onslaught will die and this wave will break.

[1] The valiant Hector, the great bulwark of Troy.

[2] I feel within my mind a civil war: on one side my reason, my senses on the other, the burning discord of which cannot be assuaged since each is sharpening his blade against the other.

Ach lasz ein Tröpflein nur von deinem Lebnstau
Erfrischen meinen Geist! Hilf, dasz ich doch nur schau
Ein Fünklein deiner Glut! So bin ich ganz erleuchtet.[1]

Gryphius' poetry, like much German verse of the period, both Protestant and Catholic, makes ready use of the language of Bible and liturgy. But an equal agony of spirit can be expressed on a purely secular topic, as by Francisco de Quevedo—a more stoical figure than Sponde—who perished in the mere contemplation of the waves of his mistress's hair. Though reduced to so small a scope, the flux is here[2] equally overwhelming; the lover, far from 'doing what he can, though powerless', suffers repeated deaths. If he finally survives it is certainly not as a hero, but 'as ashes that still retain some feeling, as a dust in which some love persists'. Quevedo is of all Baroque poets the most sensitive to the flux of time, to the imperceptible passing of the days of his life, and the gradual sapping of the weak earthen wall of the body.

Todo corto momento es paso largo
que doy, a mi pesar, en tal jornada,
pues, parado y durmiendo, siempre aguijo.[3]

Quevedo is alternately a remorseless satirist and doubter in the presence of death. Although he wrote a great deal of prose on theological subjects, he made only the most conventional statements of belief. True, his prose satire, 'Los Sueños' ('The Visions'), assumes the existence of hell, and examines its inhabitants according to their professions with a disgust that anticipates Swift. One feels no certainty, however, that Quevedo had ever received a glimpse of heaven. His most

---

[1] O measureless wisdom! O guest of pure souls! O dear fount of mercy! O consolation under harsh burdens! O rain that moistens us with a blessing in our agony! O let just a drop of your dew of life refresh my spirit! Help me to see a spark of your fire, and I shall be entirely illuminated.

[2] Sonnet, 'Afectos varios de su corazón, fluctuando en las ondas de los cabellos de Lisi.'

[3] Every short moment is a long step which I take, to my regret, on this journey [towards death] since standing or sleeping I always spur on.

poignant prayer is a hymn to the stars; and he expresses greater awe when contemplating an hour-glass than in the presence of any religious object. Just as one cannot credit Quevedo with any religious experience, so one can find nothing in his many love-poems that testifies to a true feeling for any woman. His Petrarchan elaborations seem to cover a curious sensuality and a despairing preoccupation with his own states of mind. His feeling seems to be at its strongest when he compares himself to those ruins which in other poems he has described for their own sake:

> todo soy ruinas, todo soy destrozos,
> escándalo funesto a los amantes
> que fabrican de lastima sus gozos.[1]

Quevedo, in his self-absorption, came to view all virtue as a thing of the distant past. His ideal was that age of primitive Rome, in which the victorious general, refusing the luxury of a triumph, retired in perfect simplicity to the farm from which he had been reluctantly called to save his country. Marvell points the same moral in his 'Ode upon Cromwell's Return from Ireland', in which, in defiance of history, he supposes the Republican dictator to have lived like a humble gardener until called to overthrow the monarchy,

> And cast the Kingdome old
> Into another Mold.

There is much in common between this poem and Quevedo's equally famous 'Epístola satírica y censoria' ('Satirical letter of censure'), which he addressed to the royal favourite and minister, the Conde de Olivares, and in which he implored that ambitious minister to restore his country to the age of primal simplicity. When this age had been he did not expressly point out. But once, he reminds Olivares,

---

[1] I am all ruins, all destruction, a doleful warning to lovers who make their joys out of lamentations.

Bebió la sed los arroyuelos puros;
después mostraron del carquesio a Baco
el camino los brindis mal seguros.

El rostro macilento, el cuerpo flaco,
eran recuerdo del trabajo honroso,
y honra y provecho andaban en un saco.[1]

Such had been the merits of the past. Finding nothing permanent, however, in the flux of modern existence, Quevedo saw in the ruins of ancient Rome itself only a tomb washed by the still living waters of the Tiber, which weep its destruction. Adapting a sonnet of du Bellay's, he heightens in the Baroque manner the contrast between the city that has been and the mound that remains:

Sólo el Tíber quedó; cuya corriente,
si ciudad la regó, ya sepoltura
la llora con funesto son doliente.[2]

To the Renaissance poet, the Classical past was a living reality which he sought to revive. Virgilian and Horatian echoes are to be found in the poetry of Ronsard, du Bellay, and Camões side by side with motives drawn from Petrarch. Ronsard, as we have seen, assumed the figure of a Promethean lover, and du Bellay, in one of his best-known sonnets, expressing his desire to return from Rome to the banks of his native Loire, pleaded for the good fortune of the Greek heroes Ulysses and Jason. His journey to Rome had been that of a Classical enthusiast, and at first sight even the modern city had delighted him. He felt that he had returned to the source of the culture on which he had been nourished. Beginning with the high walls and hanging gardens of Babylon, he lists

[1] Thirst drank from pure streams; afterwards unsteady toasts pointed the way to the winecup. A thin face and a lean body were the signs of honest labour, and honour and profit lay in the same sack.

[2] Only the Tiber is still here, and its current, which washed her as a city, now bewails her as a tomb with mournful sounds of grief.

all the architectural wonders of the ancient world, to conclude
that for him they are all eclipsed by the seven hills of Rome:

> Et si quelque œuvre encor digne se peut vanter
>   De marcher en ce rang, quelque plus grand faconde
> Le dira: quant à moi, pour tous je veux chanter
> Les sept coteaux Romains, sept miracles du Monde.[1]

But though du Bellay's visit began with this simple
enthusiasm, soon the contrast between Rome's past grandeurs
and the corruption of the Papal court, to which his uncle and
patron, the Cardinal du Bellay, was accredited, saddened and
disgusted him. Still, however, the reality of Rome remained
for him in those 'sacred hills and holy ruins' which alone
preserved its ancient honour:

> Sacrés coteaux, et vous saintes ruines,
> Qui le seul nom de Rome retenez,
> Vieux monuments, qui encor soutenez
> L'honneur poudreux de tant d'âmes divines.[2]

Du Bellay had initiated a theme which was developed by
many of his Baroque successors for whom the Roman past had
less reality and the ruins of the present were more obsessive.
For him the primitive grandeur of Rome was in some way
connected with the pristine simplicity of his own childhood,
from which he had fallen away into doubt, sadness, and
dissatisfaction. The Spanish antiquarian Rodrigo Caro, standing on the threshold of the Baroque world, records, in his
single poem on the ruins of Itálica, a site in the neighbourhood
of Seville on which Scipio had built a city for his legionaries, a
Rome even more distant in time and situation, the fatherland
of gods and kings,

---

[1] And if any edifice still boasts itself worthy to be included in their ranks,
some greater gossip will say so. As for me, I want to sing for everybody the
seven hills of Rome, seven miracles of the world.

[2] Sacred hills and you holy ruins which retain the unique name of
Rome, ancient monuments which still preserve the dusty honour of all those
godlike souls.

> . . . Roma, a quien queda el nombre apenas,
> ¡oh patria de los dioses y los reyes![1]

The message of Caro's poem is similar to that of Quevedo's 'Epístola', but rather more local in its loyalties. For him Trajan was more important for his Spanish birth than as a Roman emperor; and Rome was remarkable less for its own history than for having founded this colony in Spain. Quevedo, on the other hand, regrets the Roman past for its own sake, as he listens to the sad sound of Tiber bewailing its tomb.

The principal Italian poet of the Baroque age, Giambattista Marino, coming from Naples as an obscure young man to fill a minor post in an ecclesiastical establishment, was less interested to see the site of the ancient city than to 'kiss the foot of the great Shepherd' and weep for the masters of Christianity:

> e 'l sangue e l'ossa degli eroi, che tanto
> qui sudaro a fondar più stabil regno,
> lavar pietoso ed amollir col pianto![2]

Refusing even to glance at the ruins of the once imperial capital, Marino suggests by his use of the word *eroi* that the true heroes of the past were not Prometheus and Hercules, nor yet the generals and law-givers of primitive Rome, but those Christians who were martyred in the name of an other-worldly kingdom outside the stream of passing time. Even more than the Spaniard, he is the poet of the transitory scene, for whom nothing has permanent reality. Everything is decoratively beautiful, but owes its beauty entirely to man's creative imagination. Nothing appears to Marino to have permanent reality. As a scene-painter, indeed, he approximates more closely than any other poet of the Baroque age to the 'painterly style' described by Fritz Strich, and first defined by Wölfflin in words that can easily be applied to Marino: 'The

---

[1] Rome whose name scarcely survives, O country of gods and kings!
[2] And piously to bathe and steep in tears the blood and bones of the heroes, who toiled so hard to found a more lasting kingdom.

general tendency is to produce the picture no longer as a self-existing piece of the world, but as a passing show, which the spectator may enjoy only for a moment.'[1]

The poetry of Marino and his school is generally the poetry of illusion. His sonnet on the 'Instability and Fickleness of Time'[2] exhausts the commonplace of the four ages of man— or rather of woman—comparing them to the four seasons of the year. Unlike Quevedo, Marino is not haunted by the threat of decay and dissolution, but rather by unreality and evanescence. A sonnet on the death of his mistress ends as a well-turned conceit, in which Death shows the dying lady the image of its own pale face reflected in that of the poet:

> E, mentre a lato a lei piangendo er'io,
> Morte la 'nsegna sua pallida e bianca
> vincitrice spiegò sul volto mio.[3]

Marino is a master of imagery, who affected not only the lesser poets of his own country but also those of France, where he lived for eight years at the Italianate court of Louis XIII, to which he came without reputation and which he left a famous man. For in those years he had written his most sustained poem, 'L'Adone', in which he sets out to tell the story of Venus and Adonis, but loses it in a mass of descriptive digressions. Delightful in isolated passages, it cloys in its entirety. Its author appears to be in love with the pageantry of sensual existence, yet at the same time to be aware that it is in reality a passing show. A comparison between Quevedo's sonnet on his mistress's hair, already quoted, and one on a similar theme by Marino reveals the lesser urgency and the greater pictorial inventiveness of the Italian. Quevedo, characteristically, begins by exposing his own plight:

---

[1] *Principles of Art History*, translated by M. D. Hottinger (1915), p. 126.
[2] 'Dimostra la Instabilità e Varietà del Tempo' (*La Lira*, prima parte).
[3] And while I stood beside her weeping, Death showed her pale white conqueror reflected in my face.

> En crespa tempestad del oro undoso
> nada golfos de luz ardiente y pura
> mi corazón . . .[1]

and goes on to compare himself to those ancient heroes who perished by fire, by water, or by the pangs of desire. His conceits are elaborate, yet his close-packed language betrays an existential anxiety. Marino, on the other hand, is content to devote his octet to the drawing of a picture in white and gold, and does not mention his own plight until the eleventh line. Even then he does so only in conventional terms. His whole poem, indeed, is little more than a compliment turned with the greatest virtuosity:

> Onde dorati, e l'onde eran capelli,
> navicella d'avorio un dì fendea;
> una man pur d'avorio le reggea
> per questi errori prezïosi e quelli;
>   e, mentre i flutti tremolanti e belli
> con drittissimo solco dividea,
> l'òr de le rotte fila Amor cogliea,
> per formarne catene a' suoi rubelli.
>   Per l'aureo mar, che rincrespando apria
> il procelloso suo biondo tesoro,
> agitato il mio core a morte già.
>   Ricco naufragio, in cui sommerso io moro,
> poich'almen fûr, ne la tempesta mia,
> di diamante lo scoglio e 'l golfo d'oro![2]

Marino's picture begins graphically yet ends with an imprecise hyperbole. Perhaps the diamond reef is intended to

[1] In the curly tempest of wavy gold my heart swims as in gulfs of pure and burning light.

[2] Once an ivory boat was cleaving golden waves, and the waves were hair; a pure ivory hand was steering it through these precious illusions and those; and while it was dividing the rippling and lovely waves with a straight furrow, Cupid gathered the gold of the broken strands to make chains for those who rebelled against him. My heart has come to death tossed on the golden sea which curls back to reveal its turbulent fair treasure. Rich shipwreck in which I drown, since in this storm of mine the reef is diamond and the sea-depths gold!

describe the lady's forehead. This, however, would be incongruous, since we have been told that her hand is pure ivory. The diamond might stand, however, for a coronet or a jewel in her hair. From the painterly point of view, it matters very little which; all that Marino wishes to convey is that three precious substances of different colours, ivory, diamonds, and gold, are here found side by side. Quevedo, by contrast, would allow himself no such impressionism. Impelled by the feverish strength of his self-pity or self-disgust, he has turned his eyes back from his mistress upon himself, and in the final tercet sees himself in the parts first of Midas and then of Tantalus:

> Avaro y rico, y pobre en el tesoro,
> el castigo y la hambre imita a Midas,
> Tántalo en fugitivo fuente de oro.[1]

Marino's poetry, less muscular than Quevedo's, is uniformally rich and musical. A woman washing her legs is described in terms of alabaster and pearl; the water is crystal; the bath of gold and silver. When he portrays a black slave, ivory and pearl fade into darkness beside her ebony. Quevedo's 'Boda de negros' (Negroes' wedding), on the other hand, makes elaborate play with varying intensities of blackness, and ends with baleful jocosity. The outlook is black, he says, for a bridegroom whose bride is a negress, and her dowry a blank. Such unfeeling wit is foreign to Marino, who inhabits a pastoral world of birds, deer, trees, and green lawns in which ladies and peasant-girls alike may be persuaded to love, and in which the lover's worst suffering is seldom more severe than a passing disappointment. Perhaps Daphne, to escape her lover, will change into a tree, but a new nymph may be surprised in the next grove.

In Marino's world there are no eternal values, only a passing show of pageantry. The flowers smile as his mistress passes, and no victorious general of the past ever rode in a chariot comparable to the coach in which 'the light of the

[1] Greedy and rich and poor in treasure, it [my heart] copies Midas in its punishment and its hunger, Tantalus in its fleeting fountain of gold.

poet's sun' circles the heavens of love. The very exuberance and disproportion of Marino's sensual descriptions convey the quality of 'maya' or illusion that he finds in the flux of things. Yet he was able to accept this impermanence of worldly things —which so perturbed Sponde and Gryphius, and both alarmed and horrified Quevedo. In considering the state of human misery or the instability of time, he pontificates contentedly, like a lyrical Polonius, and in closing the sonnet that, after the manner of Shakespeare's speech on the seven ages of man, traces the child's fortunes from the moment when

> inghirlandò di fiori
> le sue chiome la terra[1]

to his maturity in the sweet and calm sunlight, concludes sententiously:

> Or giunta la stagion fredda e canuta,
> di rughe il volto, il crin di neve ha pieno.
> Così stato ed età qua giù si muta![2]

It was possible for a poet to remain unperturbed by the sound of 'Times winged Charriot', which so concerned Marvell. But Marino was the sanguine exception among the time-haunted poets of his day, whose obsessive mood was one of anxiety before the remorseless flow of the days.

---

[1] Earth garlanded his head with flowers.
[2] Now comes the cold and hoary season, the face is full of wrinkles, the locks of snow. Thus state and age are always changing here!

2

Desert and charnel-house

THE Baroque was not the first age in which western man was haunted by the image of death, and continuously reminded of the vanity of all earthly achievements. In all epochs of purely destructive—as opposed to heroic—wars, and of social upheavals, such thoughts have arisen in the minds of those sensitive to the deep currents of events, and have been expressed in the painting, the window-glass, the popular iconography, the sermons, the religious drama and the poetry of the day. At the same time there has been a growth of individual mysticism, a resolute endeavour by a religious minority to turn its back on the world, and a corresponding decline in general morals and the efficiency of institutional religion. Common men have envisaged, and orthodox and heretic preachers alike have prophesied, the imminent collapse of Christianity, a spectacular growth of the powers of evil, and even the approaching end of the world.

The fourteenth century, which saw the Black Death and the devastation of France in the Hundred Years War, and which was also the age of the Rhineland and English mystics —Suso, Tauler, Ruysbroeck, Juliana of Norwich, and the anonymous author of *The Cloud of Unknowing*—presents many parallels with the age we are examining, as does our own age also. But whereas we stand too near to our present collapse of values to see it in sufficient perspective, between the fourteenth and the seventeenth centuries a firm comparison can be drawn. In the field of poetry both attained a high degree of formalism and artificiality. The ballade and rondeau, which were perfected in fourteenth-century France, predominated to much the same extent in their day as the sonnet and the looser Italian verse forms in the age of the Baroque. Novelty of form was rare, and the simple strength of feeling even rarer, though the poetry of the Baroque age is strong with emotions that are none the less clear for being disguised or even half suppressed on account of the censorship of free thought that accompanied the Counter-Reformation. The quality that the poets both of the fourteenth and the seventeenth centuries pursued most anxiously was originality of metaphor and treatment. In both the balanced viewpoint was rare; strangeness and exaggeration were eagerly pursued, and detail tended to obscure the firm outline or argument of a poem.

The French critic J. Rousset, one of the most able analysts of the Baroque in post-war Europe, has postulated[1] the survival of fourteenth-century ideas, or at least their reappearance in almost identical form, as a leading constituent of the Baroque style. Certainly the motif of the constant presence of death is common to the writings of both ages. In the fourteenth century it frequently takes the form of the 'Ubi sunt', with its lament for the passing of all heroes and of all the pageantry of earth. Appearing in vernacular poetry at the beginning of the thirteenth century in the 'Vers de la Mort' of the Cistercian monk Hélinand, it culminates on the threshold of the Renaissance in Villon's famous 'Ballade des Dames du Temps Jadis', with its refrain, 'Mais où sont les neiges d'antan?'

Formally, however, there is no connection between the 'Ubi sunt' and the charnel-house poetry of the seventeenth century. The ballade had died and was not revived; the *coplas* survived but were never again used for such serious purposes. If the death's head once more became the subject of poetry it was because the outward circumstances of the seventeenth century were similar to those of the fourteenth.

The Renaissance had been a time of war, but the Italian campaigns of the emperors and the kings of France and Spain had been conducted on the heroic scale. The new wars of religion, however, were sordidly destructive. No ideal cause was served, and the best men, like Montaigne, moved into

[1] See *La Littérature de l'Age Baroque en France*.

positions of agonized neutrality. Once more, as in the Hundred Years War, whole countries were devastated. Once more men were all too frequently reminded of the likelihood of sudden and violent death by epidemic, at the hands of marauders or private bands, which were so much more remorseless than royal armies, or by the accidents of power-politics in times of disputed sovereignty.

The seventeenth century saw the menace of the death's head, though in a new form; and the revival of mysticism which it also witnessed failed to repeat exactly the pattern of the fourteenth century. Now it had two shapes: the Catholic life of dedicated activity after the example of the reforming convent-founding Santa Teresa, and the Protestant and theosophical life of passivity, in the spirit of Jakob Boehme. Both affected the poetry of the age, and both alike were, in essence, symptoms of reaction against a profound disillusionment. Whereas the fourteenth century had seen the ideal of the universal church finally perish in schism and worldliness, the seventeenth saw the Renaissance's hopes of a civilized secular society ruined by civil and religious wars.

The Baroque age, being thus especially aware of the presence of death, differed, as has been said, from the Renaissance in its attitude to Time. Fritz Strich, defining this difference in relation to the painted portrait, reinforces some of the points made in my last chapter and touches also on the subject of this one.

> One sees in Rembrandt's men [he says] that they have a past and a future, for they live in Time. One sees, one realizes, that one day they must die, because death is immanent in their lives, it is innate in them . . . A portrait by Raphael, on the other hand, takes a man out of Time, and removes him into the sphere of Timelessness.[1]

Not only was Rembrandt aware that his sitters were on their way to death, and that he was portraying not their eternal being but a brief moment in their lives, a section of

[1] Op. cit., p. 256.

the road from birth to the grave, but in his self-portraits he developed the idea even more thoroughly, noting a whole series of temporary appearances and passing expressions, all of which went to the composition of a single man's life. He recorded their monumentality as imperishable moments caught in the lightning-flash of his self-perception, but also their fleetingness. 'This is not I,' he seems to say, 'I have passed on.'

For the Renaissance painter or poet, the permanent seemed to triumph over the transitory. Love, even when unfulfilled, could conquer death; the pictured greatness of doge or senator outlasted the fever of his death-bed and the panoply of his funeral procession. Buried and entombed, he yet lived on in his portrait. Michelangelo, architect, sculptor, painter, and poet, saw in his love for a mortal being an aspiration towards the 'form of universal beauty', and believed that a relationship which on earth depended on the senses would become more perfect, through death, in heaven:

> Io dico, c'a chi vive quel che muore
> quetar non può desir, nè par s'aspetti
> l'eterno al tempo, ove altri cangia il pelo.
> Voglia sfrenata il senso è, non amore,
> che l'alma uccide; e 'l nostro fa perfetti
> gli'amici qui, ma più per morte in cielo.[1]

The key to Michelangelo's meaning clearly depends on his use of the word death, which can be interpreted on two levels. Do these last lines of the sonnet 'Non vider gli occhi miei . . .' speak of physical death and the birth of a renewed and purer friendship in another place beyond the grave? Or is 'l'eterno' an experience attainable in this life by the relinquishing of temporal and sensual desires? Is Michelangelo speaking of

---

[1] I say that what is mortal cannot still the desire of one who is alive, nor does eternity seem to wait upon time, in which the skins of others change. The senses lead not to love but to unbridled desire, which kills the soul; and our love makes perfect friendships here, but more perfect still, through death, in heaven.

self-transcendence with the consequent death of the old Adam? One is confronted with similar questions on reading certain sonnets of Shakespeare, among them:

> How like a winter hath my absence been
> From thee, the pleasure of the fleeting year!

The object of the address can be a loved person, an adulated patron, or, perhaps with greater likelihood, a level of existence no sooner savoured than lost. Death and loss may be both personal and spiritual; and much Renaissance poetry besides that of Michelangelo and Shakespeare bestrides these two levels in the neo-Platonic manner. The Spaniard Garcilaso de la Vega, who was the first successfully to acclimatize the new measures to the Peninsula, speaks in Petrarchan tones more sober than those of the Italians of the loss of his love and of the consequent lack of direction on the path of life. The latter image occurs in at least two of his sonnets, the first of which, 'Por ásperos caminos he llegado', proclaims not only a total acceptance of death—in whichever sense we interpret the word—but a bluntly objective admission of his failure both in love and in his worldly career. Such I am, he confesses, that with death already beside me I still seek new guidance from my life:

> Mas tal estoy, que con la muerte al lado
> busco de mi vivir consejo nuevo;
> y conozco el mejor y el peor apruebo,
> o por costumbre mala o por mi hado.[1]

The pessimism of those lines contrasts with the more hopeful ending of a second sonnet, related to the first by the common situation of the 'rough roads' or 'desert place', both of which distantly recall the opening lines of the *Inferno*:

[1] But I am such that with death at my side I still seek new guidance from my life; knowing the better course, I approve the worse, either because of bad habits or through fate.

A la entrada de un valle, en un desierto,
do nadie atravesaba ni se vía,
vi que con estrañeza un can hacía
estremos de dolor con desconcierto;
    ahora suelta el llanto al cielo abierto,
ora va rastreando por la vía;
camina, vuelve, para, y todavía
quedaba desmayado como muerto.
    Y fué que se apartó de su presencia
su amo, y no le hallaba, y esto siente;
mirad hasta dó llega el mal de ausencia.
    Movióme a compasión ver su accidente;
díjele lastimado: 'Ten paciencia,
que yo alcanzo razón, y estoy ausente.'[1]

The surprising shift of significance in the last lines is
prematurely Baroque. The poet has become the dog's master.
While still, in the person of the dog, deploring his lost love and
his sense of worldly dereliction, he now presents himself as in
an other-worldly or spiritual sense absent, if only for a while,
because he is pursuing a higher reason, from which he will
bring comfort to his other and lower self. The dog lost in a
vast and trackless desert is a symbol of anxiety; and the broken
insistence of the language also, particularly in the opening
quatrain, anticipates the disquiet of the seventeenth century.
It is quite foreign to the more *reasonable* and balanced styles of
Michelangelo, Ronsard, and Shakespeare. Garcilaso, a gentleman soldier, comparable in externals to Sir Philip Sidney,
like him perished prematurely in a minor battle. Unlike
Sidney, however, he hated the life of soldier and courtier, and
longed only to be at peace. His pastoral poetry is rich in

[1] At the entrance of a valley, in a desert which no one crossed and
where no one could be seen, I saw a dog in bewilderment giving vent to
extremes of wild anguish. Sometimes he howls aloud to the open sky, and
sometimes drags himself along the road. He goes on, turns round, stops and
is all the time as feeble as a dead man. It was because his master had gone
away and he could not find him, and this grieved him. See how severe the
pains of absence can be! His plight moved me to compassion, and I said to
him in grief: 'Be patient, for I am following reason, and am absent only for
a while.'

sharply etched pictures of the Spanish countryside to which he longed to retire. His Arcadia was like Marvell's garden of inner peace rather than Sidney's conventional land of romance. It was the embodiment of a private paradise into which he never found admission. Though the first poet of the Spanish Renaissance, he was already afflicted with the 'existential' bewilderment of the age of Quevedo.

In Spain the Baroque anxiety developed steadily and prematurely throughout the Renaissance. Garcilaso's successor, admirer and editor, the Sevillan poet Fernando de Herrera, a cleric whose loves were almost certainly Platonic, likewise found himself in a desert place, and in the sonnet 'Por altos bosques voy' proclaimed a grief that resembles Garcilaso's:

> Los ojos alço y veo un gran desierto
> lleno de orror, de espinos mal compuesto;
> desmayo en un intenso dolor puesto
> y a mi salud no hallo passo abierto.[1]

The horror embodied by Garcilaso in the symbol of the lost dog is placed by Herrera in the thorn-choked desert itself. Herrera, who celebrated his country's political greatness in 'state poems' of eloquent grandeur, and who mourned the defeat of Don Sebastião of Portugal by the Moors in a funeral poem second to none of its age, viewed his own fate with a despair even greater than Garcilaso's. Despair was gaining ground. The refusal to look outwards any more, of which Philip II's gaunt, introverted monastery-palace of El Escorial was the architectural symbol, had become general in Spain even before her power had reached its height. With the deliberate suppression of Erasmus's influence, optimism disappeared at the same time as freedom of thought. The Church triumphed; and no poet could any longer find his own way to salvation.

In those countries where Protestantism and Erasmian

[1] I lift up my eyes and see a great desert, full of horror, choked with evil thorns, and I faint in an access of intense grief, and can find no way open to my salvation.

thought survived, the lapse into existential anxiety came more slowly, and under pressure of violent events rather than of thought-censorship. Though Du Bellay's 'Songe', which follows his 'Antiquitéz de Rome', contains elements that were worked up by later French poets into scenes of true horror—it is more fanciful than menacing. There is no fear of death in his description of the destruction of Caesar's ashes in their grandly architectural tomb:

> Digne tombeau d'une si digne cendre[1]

and only the most conventional moral accompanies the lightning-flash which strikes it:

> Là, rien ne dure au monde que torment!
> Je vis du ciel la tempête descendre,
> Et foudroyer ce brave monument.[2]

Du Bellay and Ronsard regret the passing of beauty, the onset of old age, and sigh to be in some other place or time. But they betray neither horror nor anxiety. True horror did not enter French poetry until the religious wars had reached their most sordid epoch. It first appears in the work of the Protestant Sponde, already quoted, and of the precocious young Catholic Jean-Baptiste Chassignet, who had composed his collection of 434 sonnets, 'Les Mespris de la Vie et Consolation contre la Mort', by the age of twenty-three.

The Spanish poets of the Renaissance, lost in their desert of grief, spoke in metaphor of bewilderment and the death of the spirit. Though they paid for their immunity by a speedy fossilization of thought, they were spared the long nastiness of civil war. French poets of the late sixteenth century, on the other hand, were frequently confronted with violent death in all its purposeless horror. The Spaniard did not brood on the *auto-da-fé* which took place in his streets, since a Jew or relapsed

---

[1] Worthy tomb of such worthy ashes.
[2] Alas, nothing lasts in the world except torture! I saw the storm descend from the sky and strike this brave monument.

heretic was in a state of sin, and therefore hardly human. His execution, therefore, was no more than a hygienic method of saving his soul. In the French civil wars, on the other hand, members of the same family were to be found in opposite parties, and slaughter was a shocking occurrence to reasonable men in both camps.

Using the imagery of the sick-bed, the grave, and the charnel-house, these French poets dwelt on the spectacle of corruption with fascinated resignation, to express which they resorted at times to an un-Petrarchan homeliness of language. This, however, was not altogether an innovation. One finds it already in these last verses of Ronsard which were written on his sick-bed under the stress of pain and sleeplessness. It is true that when he apostrophizes the long nights of winter he remembers them first for their mythological associations and addresses them as daughters of Cocytus and sisters of Enceladus, the giant who was born of Earth. Yet the end of the sonnet which begins with this Renaissance apostrophe is as tortured as the direct and realistic poetry of his Baroque successors:

> Seize heures pour le moins je meurs les yeux ouverts,
> Me tournant, me virant de droit et de travers,
> Sur l'un, sur l'autre flanc; je tempête, je crie,
>   Inquiet, je ne puis en un lieu me tenir,
> J'appelle en vain le Jour, et la Mort je supplie,
> Mais elle fait la sourde et ne veut pas venir.[1]

Ronsard's almost tender portrait of death in his last line is, however, characteristic of the Renaissance rather than the Baroque age, which habitually pictured it not as a woman but as a sexless skull. It is in the first of this set of five sonnets on sickness and death that Ronsard most closely anticipates Sponde's poems on the same theme.

---

[1] For sixteen hours at least I have been dying with open eyes, turning and twisting to the right and across the bed, first on one side and then on the other. I storm and cry, and am too restless to stay in one position. In vain I call for day and pray for death. But she pretends to be deaf and will not come.

Je n'ai plus que les os, un squelette je semble,
Décharné, dénervé, démusclé, dépoulpé,[1]

he observes with a clinical exactness which was afterwards
practised by the equally morbid poet Chassignet. Ronsard,
however, up to this last moment, was not obsessed by death,
though he was certainly mindful that old age would destroy
his own and his mistress's charm and vigour. It was not until
it haunted his last nights that he let it invade his poetry.
Sponde, on the other hand, brooded constantly on death. It is
present in all his mature poetry. Unlike Ronsard, who calls
on it (or her) only to rescue him from his anguish, Sponde
celebrates death's triumphs in a manner that recalls the
fourteenth century. His buoyant rhythms indeed suggest that
death makes an almost sensuous appeal to him. This is certainly
true of his second sonnet 'sur le mesme subject de la Mort':

Mais si faut-il mourir, et la vie orgueilleuse,
Qui brave de la mort, sentira ses fureurs,
Les Soleils hâleront ces journalières fleurs,
Et le temps crévera cette ampoulle venteuse.

Ce beau flambeau, qui lance une flamme fumeuse
Sur le vert de la cire éteindra ses ardeurs.
L'huile de ce tableau ternira ses couleurs,
Et ces flots se rompront à la rive écumeuse.

J'ai vu ces clairs éclairs passer devant mes yeux,
Et le tonnerre encor qui gronde dans les Cieux,
Où d'une, ou d'autre part, éclatera l'orage.

J'ai vu fondre la neige, et ses torrents tarir,
Ces lions rugissants je les ai vu sans rage,
Vivez, hommes, vivez, mais si faut-il mourir.[2]

[1] I have nothing left but bone, I look like a skeleton, fleshless, without
nerves, muscles or covering to my bones.

[2] And yet we must die, and proud life, which defies death, will feel its
fury; suns will wither these flowers of a day and time will burst this bladder
of wind. This fine candle which darts a smoky flame will burn out its heat
on the green of the wax. The oils of this picture will dim their colours, and
these waves will break on the foamy shore. I have seen the bright lightning
pass before my eyes, and the thunder also rumbling in the heavens, in which
the storm will break from one quarter or another. I have seen the snow melt
and its streams run dry. I have seen those roaring lions calmed of their rage.
Live, men, live, but yet you must die.

As in his sonnet on the flux of the world, already quoted, Sponde's prevailing mood is of mingled excitement and anxiety. But here the visual power is much stronger. The images have a nightmare quality which recalls that of Garcilaso in his desert sonnets. The break with Ronsard and the Pléiade is complete. A further comparison with du Bellay's 'Songe', which ostensibly set out to convey the urgency of dream, shows how much less compelling is the earlier poet's pace. The opening of his fifth sonnet,

> Je vis un fier Torrent, dont les flots écumeux
> Rongeaient les fondements d'une vieille ruine,[1]

conveys no such immediacy as do Sponde's drying watercourses, which he compares by a surprisingly Baroque—or disproportionate—image to roaring lions that have been tamed. Du Bellay's vision, by contrast, contains no surprises, and Sponde himself in this respect falls behind the later *libertin* poet, Théophile de Viau, who to suggest disorder in Nature moves in his well-known Ode from the natural observation of its first baleful line,

> Un corbeau devant moi croasse[2]

to the nightmare nonsense with which its second verse opens:

> Ce ruisseau remonte en sa source,
> Un bœuf gravit sur un clocher,
> Le sang coule de ce rocher . . .[3]

The progressive distortion, from du Bellay's vision of a 'proud torrent', by way of Sponde's watercourses like 'roaring lions', to de Viau's stream which baldly defies Nature and flows

---

[1] I saw a fierce torrent, whose yeasty waves sapped the foundations of an ancient ruin.

[2] A crow caws in front of me.

[3] This stream flows back to its source, an ox climbs a bell-tower, blood flows from this rock.

back to its source, is a measure of the growing violence of Baroque imagery.

Sponde's sonnet assembles all the conventional portents of death: the withering of flowers, the bursting of a bladder or bubble, the breaking of a storm, the roll of thunder or lightning-flash, and the drying of a stream, yet he gives them an individual stamp. Moreover there is a compelling and elegiac beauty in his third line,

Les Soleils hâleront ces journalières fleurs,

which, like other striking felicities of Baroque poetry, not only looks backward to Ronsard but forward to the resounding phraseology of the Romantics. Sponde's two further analogies, however, are strictly of their time. For they are based on objective observation of a kind that was quite foreign to the Pléiade, and did not occur in nineteenth-century poetry until the time of 'Les Fleurs du Mal'.

The guttering of his unsnuffed candle-flame in its green wax and the loss of brightness in a picture that has been varnished are Sponde's own images, though the former recalls the candlelit visions of the contemporary painter Georges de la Tour, for whom the candle's bright light had a similar fascination, perhaps because, like the approach of death, it rendered the flesh transparent.

Imagery which resembles Sponde's, but is even more gruesomely realistic, prevails in the far more copious production of the Besançon doctor's son Jean-Baptiste Chassignet who, after abandoning poetry, occupied an important legal post in his native town and devoted himself to regional history and to a verse paraphrase of the Bible. The sonnets of his youth have only lately achieved publication. They take the form of a long series of meditations on the subject of mortality, the intention of which is to give the reader a contempt for life and to console him for the certainty of death. Chassignet developed many of the Baroque commonplaces on the subject of the brevity and uncertainty of our earthly existence. He

treated in greater detail than Sponde the comparison of man's
life to a bursting bubble:

> Qu'est-ce de votre vie? une bouteille molle
> Qui s'enfle dessus l'eau quand le ciel fait pleuvoir,
> Et se perd aussitôt comme elle se fait voir,
> S'entrebrisant à l'heurt d'une moindre bricole:[1]

The picture of this bubble thrown up and burst by the fall
of the next rain-drop beside it speaks of an even closer natural
observation than Sponde's. We seem to see this tiny event in
the magnified detail of a cinema close-up in slow motion.
Chassignet secures the same fascination in his reader by
drawing freely and in similar detail on memories of his father's
surgery. Encouraging a friend to confront death boldly, he
reminds him of the variety of diseases from which he may
suffer:

> Tantôt la crampe aux pieds, tantôt la goutte aux mains,
> Le muscle, le tendon, et le nerf te travaille;
> Tantôt un pleurésie te livre la bataille,
> Et la fièvre te point de ses traits inhumains;
> Tantôt l'âpre gravelle épaissit en tes reins . . .[2]

In another sonnet he points the moral by an anatomical
description of a rotting corpse, modelled, as has been noted, on
some lines by Ronsard:

> Mortel, pense quel est dessous la couverture
> D'un charnier mortuaire un corps mangé de vers,
> Décharné, dénervé, où les os découvers,
> Dépoulpés, dénoués, délaissent leur jointure:

[1] What is your life? a soft bubble that swells on the water when the
heavens send rain and disappears as soon as it is seen, bursting under the
impact of the slightest jar.

[2] Sometimes cramp in the feet, sometimes in the hands, a muscle, a
tendon, a nerve pains you; sometimes a pleurisy attacks you, and fever
pricks you with its cruel shafts. Sometimes sharp gravel forms in your
kidneys. . . .

> Ici l'une des mains tombe de pourriture,
> Les yeux d'autre côté détournés à l'envers
> Se distillent en glaire . . .[1]

Chassignet's horror of death is not so great as Sponde's. Despite his wealth of hideous details, his rhythms are less agitated and his intellectual curiosity is certainly wider. Everything that he sees and hears is liable to remind him of mortality. An anecdote from history, the contemplation of some animal, fish or flower: all remind him of the inevitability of the death-bed. Man's only hope is that, like the act of birth for the mother, death will be over quickly, and that it brings the key to eternal life. There is a hope greater than Sponde's in his childbirth sonnet which begins clinically:

> La femme grosse endure une extrême souffrance
> Sur le point d'accoucher, mais en moins d'un moment
> Elle met en oubli après l'enfantement,
> De son travail passé la dure violence.[2]

Perhaps tiring of the contemplation of death, perhaps because he accepted his own lesson of consolation, Chassignet, while still a young man, turned away from poetry, and, like Rimbaud, though with greater success, devoted the rest of his life to his career.

The charnel-house preoccupation of the French poets towards the end of the wars of religion was matched by a similar preoccupation among the Germans during their own somewhat later Thirty Years War. The prolonged meditation of the poet and dramatist Andreas Gryphius, their outstanding writer of this age, on his visit to a churchyard and ossuary, his

[1] Mortal, consider what a corpse looks like beneath the blanket in a mortuary, worm-eaten, fleshless, nerveless, and with its bones stripped bare, no longer connected and falling apart. Here one of the hands is rotting, and there the eyes, turning inwards, are distilling slime.

[2] The pregnant woman undergoes extreme suffering as she brings the child forth, but in less than a moment after the birth, she forgets the severity of her labours.

'Gedanken über den Kirchhof und Ruhestatt der Verstorbenen', catalogues the rotting limbs and bones that he saw with an enthusiastic exactness worthy of the French doctor's son. There is, however, a certain naïveté about his cheerful rhythms and the briskness with which he assembles his grisly details—a naïveté foreign both to Chassignet, who though sometimes clumsy was the heir to a longer poetic tradition, and also to Gryphius himself when writing at his best. The opening question of the quotation that follows is somewhat emptily rhetorical. Yet the passage grows in power as it proceeds:

> Was nützt der Schulterblätter Paar?
> Der Arme Rohr ist sonder Stärke
> Und, was des Menschen eigen war,
> Die Hand, das Werkzeug höchster Werke,
> Das See und Land und Luft bewegt,
> Und aller Thurst sich unterwunden,
> Ist durch des Grabes Macht entbunden,
> Zerstückt, entädert und zerlegt.[1]

Gryphius dwells in incessant detail on the intestines that burst through the skin, the decomposition of the nose and the worms stirring behind the eyes. One feels that he luxuriates too freely in the spectacle of corruption to be truly concerned with his moral, that man should bid farewell to the world and travel from death into life. The poem written on his own sick-bed, 'Tränen in schwerer Krankheit', is briefer and more moving.

Compared with Chassignet and Gryphius, John Donne in his poems on death is sparing in physical imagery, and more effective in its use. They are preoccupied with the spectacle of corruption, he with its significance in a certain situation, as a symbol rather than an obsession. He is not merely a realist, he challenges Nature in the name of the intellect: a quality

---

[1] Of what use are the two shoulder-blades? The shaft of the arm has lost its strength and, what was peculiar to man, the hand, creator of finest works, which moves sea and land and air, having attempted all desires, is delivered by the power of the grave, dismembered, stripped of its veins and broken up.

seriously lacking both in Chassignet and Gryphius. In 'The Funeral' he states in defiance of all logic that a lock of his mistress's hair, thought of as a saint's relic (though saints' relics were no longer reverenced in Protestant England), will keep his body from dissolution:

> For 'tis my outward soule,
> Viceroy to that, which then to heaven being gone,
>   Will leave this to controule
> And keep these limbes, her Provinces, from dissolution.

The effect of Donne's poem is to lift carnal objects into the world of ideas. The limbs, whose decay is so studiously recorded by Chassignet and Gryphius, are here seen in their dependence on a higher principle, the soul. For Donne even the decay of the flesh is a metaphysical proposition. The poets of the French and German Baroque, on the other hand, though they call on God to rescue them from the pit of corruption, find no evidence of His presence there. Heaven and earth are separate realms, and they see no principle that unites them, other than the single descent of Christ, which is seldom their subject. Viewing death and even resurrection in their purely carnal aspects, Chassignet sees himself confronted by a corporeal angel, or shown from a high place that there is nothing permanent beneath the vault of the sky. In either case, the poem's accent is on the senses. Donne, on the other hand, reasons from sensuality to the Scholastic world of ideas, in which life, death, and resurrection have each their place on the plane of emotional thought. Donne's influence remained strong in English poetry of the Baroque, which—unlike Jacobean drama, with its Italianate plots—was not deflected into any charnel-house exaggeration, perhaps because the Civil War of Roundhead and Cavalier caused little slaughter and destruction.

The Italians, too, being spared both the Continental Wars of Religion and the rule of intellectual bigotry which ruined Spain, tended to treat death in an objective way as the culmination of human misfortunes rather than to luxuriate in its physical horrors. Marino and his many interesting followers, who are still little known even in Italy, being intellectually less tough than their English contemporaries, tend to dwell on the sensual rather than the metaphysical aspects of experience. Marino's sonnet on the subject of human misfortune ('Tratta delle Miserie umane') is coolly objective:

> Chiude alfin le sue spoglie angusto sasso,
> ratto così, che sospirando io dico:
> —Da la cuna a la tomba è un breve passo![1]

Though Marino piled up the horrors in the second book of 'La Strage degli Innocenti' ('The Massacre of the Innocents'), a long early poem of which Richard Crashaw translated the first book, he was not death-obsessed in the manner of Gryphius and Chassignet. The horrors of his 'Massacre' are on the whole less impressive than the wealth of sensual detail in his more mature poem 'L'Adone'.

Nor are the verses put into the mouth of Death by Marino's friend and follower Claudio Achillini much more than a conventional *memento mori*:

> questi occhi cavernosi,
> de gli ultimi spaventi umidi alberghi,
> queste squallide rughe
> che mi solcan le guancie,
> e queste falce adunca,
> fanno tragica fede,
> timidi spettatori,
> che la Morte presente a voi ragiona.[2]

The Marinist poet, Ciro de Pers, uses an attack of the stone, a fit subject for Chassignet, as the pretext for a series of punning conceits in which he laments the hardness of his fate:

---

[1] A narrow stone in the end conceals its spoils, so swiftly that I say with a sigh: 'From the cradle to the grave is but a brief step.'

[2] These hollow eyes, moist homes of the final terrors, these sad wrinkles that furrow my cheeks, and this curved scythe, offer tragic testimony, O timid spectators, that instant death is addressing you.

Io ben posso chiamar mia sorte dura,
s'ella è di pietra. Ha preso a lapidarmi
de la parte di dentro la natura.[1]

Another follower of Marino, Pier Francesco Paoli, treating the
subject rather more seriously, sees his sufferings from the same
disease as an aid to his eternal salvation. Yet he too cannot
resist a final conceit in which he pictures himself as a penitent
Sisyphus flying up, with his heavy stone, into Paradise:

e tutto lieto il cor, se mesto il viso,
m'inalzerò con grave sasso a volo,
Sisifo penitente, al paradiso.[2]

The Baroque preoccupation extended beyond the death
and decay of the body to an equally gloomy prognosis of
society. Not only did the men of that age see corruption
confronting them on every side, but they had lost all hope in
the present and future. What was good, as has been said, lay
in the past, in an epoch of greater rectitude and simplicity,
which some might equate with the times of the Roman
Republic, others with a moment of their own nation's expansion and vigour in the more immediate past. Quevedo, in his
'Epístola satírica y censoria', drew a parallel between the years
of Rome's early greatness and the Spain of his grandfather's
day, in which he believed the stoic virtues to have prevailed:

Que el vientre, entonces bien disciplinado,
buscó satisfacción y no hartura,
y estaba la garganta sin pecado.

Del mayor infanzón de aquella pura
república de grandes hombres era
una vaca sustento y armadura.

---

[1] I may well call my fate hard since it is of stone. It has made Nature
stone me from within.

[2] And with a joyful heart if a sad face, I shall fly up to paradise with my
heavy stone, a penitent Sisyphus.

No había venido, al gusto lisonjera,
la pimienta arrugada, ni del clavo
la adulación fragante forastera.[1]

Quevedo was a bitter man, to whom Truth was 'the tongue of a harsh god'—

que es lengua la verdad de Dios severo

—which he felt himself compelled to wag on every occasion. It is as hard to believe that he really attributed the decline of Spain to the importation of foreign spices, which were surely necessary since Spanish meat has always been tough and tasteless, as to credit his expressed hope that the new favourite would restore virtues neglected by the old. The confidence with which he begins his poem is over-determined. His assertion that a brave man must now speak out is, in fact, a form of personal defiance. No minister could at that late hour put the clock back. Freedom of speech had disappeared from Spain with Cervantes. Quevedo's part was to protest and repine. Even as he had sighed over the ruins of Rome, so in another sonnet he resigned himself without hope or reservation to the spectacle of his country's ruin:

Miré los muros de la patria mía,
si un tiempo fuertes, ya desmoronados,
de la carrera de la edad cansados
por quien caduca ya su valentía.[2]

True though it was, one cannot take Quevedo's prognosis as entirely objective. By the conclusion of this sonnet, indeed,

[1] For the stomach, well disciplined in those days, sought repletion rather than surfeit, and the gullet was without sin. One cow gave food and leather enough for the greatest prince in that pure nation of great men. The wrinkled pepper and the fragrant, foreign flattery of the clove had not yet come to tickle the palate.

[2] I looked on the walls of my fatherland, once so strong but now mouldering away, weary with the passage of time, by which their valour is now decaying.

he had come to consider his own case, and to draw the parallel
between himself and his country:

> Vencida de la edad sentí mi espada,
> y no hallé cosa en que poner los ojos
> que no fuese recuerdo de la muerte.[1]

Ruins, whether of Rome or of some Spanish city, reminded
Quevedo not only of their past glories but also of his own
approaching death. His contemporary Rodrigo Caro, on the
other hand, gazing on the ruins of Itálica, showed a greater
sense of history. Standing among its overgrown mounds, he
called up the vision of its amphitheatre packed for a grand
spectacle. In his ears there still rang the cry

> ¡cayó Itálica![2]

If this city was Time's laughing-stock it was, in his view, as
much on account of her former greatness as of her present
desolation. His values were Christian. The vision that he
sought was not of a naked swordsman confronting the wild
beasts in her arena, but of her legendary martyr Gerontius,
whose sacrifice alone made her great.

> ¡Goza en las tuyas sus reliquias bellas
> para envidia del mundo y las estrellas![3]

he concludes. The rise and fall of cities is to him nothing
compared with the eternal truth for which this martyr died.

For other poets, however, the fall of a building or a
city was a sign of God's anger at the sins of men. Such
was the moral drawn by the Silesian Christian Hofmann
von Hofmannswaldau from the collapse of the church of St

---

[1] I felt my sword conquered by the years, and found nothing to look upon
that was not a reminder of death.

[2] Italica has fallen!

[3] Enjoy his fair remains on your own, and be the envy of the world and
the stars.

C

Elizabeth at Breslau, which he recounted in spectacular and onomatopoeic detail:

> Mit starkem Krachen brach der Bau des Herren ein,
> Die Pfeiler gaben nach, die Balken muszten biegen,
> Die Ziegel wollten sich nicht mehr zusammenfügen:
> Es trennte Kalk von Kalk und risz sich Stein von Stein.[1]

We are reminded of Chassignet's vision of the human frame, with flesh falling away from bone and the bones themselves breaking apart. Hofmannswaldau, however, although like Chassignet a Catholic, does not conclude with a dogmatic platitude to the effect that life not death is the cause of our misfortunes,

> La vie, et non la mort, de nos maux est la cause,

but with a warning placed in the mouth of the Old Testament God of the Protestants:

> Die Sünde kommt von dir, das Scheitern kommt von Gott,
> Und ist dein Herze Stein und dein Gemüte tot,
> So müssen dich itzund die toten Steine lehren.[2]

The fall of a single church was as nothing to the wreckage of a whole country devastated by thirty years of war. Quevedo could bitterly deplore the decline of his country's greatness, and Hofmannswaldau brood over the portents of a single disaster. Gryphius, on the other hand, invoking neither God nor man, and weeping no tears for himself, narrated in his sonnet 'Tränen des Vaterlandes' the whole list of evils from which Germany suffered. Now he had no need to visit a mortuary in order to arouse the desired lugubrious feelings. He had only to look outside his door:

[1] With a loud crash the Lord's house collapsed, the pillars gave way, the beams were forced to bend, the bricks no longer held together, mortar parted from mortar and stone tore away from stone.

[2] The sin is yours, the destruction comes from God, and if your heart is stone and your spirit dead, the dead stones will have to teach you now.

Die Türme stehn in Glut, die Kirch' ist umgekehret,
Das Rathaus liegt im Graus, die Starken sind zerhaun,
Die Jungfern sind geschändt, und wo wir hin nur schaun,
Ist Feuer, Pest und Tod, der Herz und Geist durchfähret
    Hier durch die Schanz und Stadt rinnt allzeit frisches
                               Blut,
Dreimal sind schon sechs Jahr, als unser Ströme Flut,
Von Leichen fast verstopft, sich langsam fortgedrungen.[1]

The charnel-house vision of the Baroque age was here justified. Reality matched itself with the most morbid of imaginations. Just as in the present century the nightmare imagery of surrealism was developed in advance of actual events, or at least at some distance from them, but proved no more than naturalistic in Madrid or Warsaw or London under bombardment or in the Paris of the Resistance, so the charnel-house, at first the product of the subjective imagination at work on the brooding evil of the times, found its objective embodiment in the wintry fields and devastated towns of a starving and plague-stricken Germany.

---

[1] The towers are on fire, the church is cast down, the town hall lies in ruins, the strong are maimed, the virgins are raped, and wherever we look there is nothing but fire, plague, and death, that pierces heart and mind. Here through the bulwarks and the town ever fresh blood is running. Eighteen years ago the water of our rivers slowly found its way past the corpses that almost blocked it.

3

Sacred and profane love

'THOUGH the stair of love is very noble and few attain to it,' says the poet and future Cardinal Pietro Bembo, in Castiglione's *Courtier*, 'yet it cannot be called perfect . . . For since at this early stage love enjoys the aid of the senses, it is not completely purged of gross darkness.' After this classic exposition of the Platonic theory the author, still speaking through the mouth of the Italian Renaissance poet, goes on to recommend that the courtier, or ideal gentleman, whom he is addressing, 'shall not lose his wits, as he would were he to consider bodily beauty alone, but shall gain their true use by contemplating that beauty which is to be seen with the eyes of the mind'. This purging of sensuality, which Castiglione compares to the fire which consumed Hercules on the summit of Mount Oeta, and to Moses' burning bush, 'doubles', in his belief, 'the grace and happiness of those souls that are worthy to see it, when they forsake the lowly earth and fly up into heaven'.

This Platonic theory of love, superimposed on the Petrarchan convention, which in its turn derives from the mediaeval principle of Courtly Love—itself distantly Platonic in origin—informs almost all the amatory poetry of the Renaissance. Though celebrating, at one level, a passion, either fulfilled or unfulfilled, the poets of this age invariably spoke also, simultaneously and at a higher level, of the beloved as a reflection of the divine. Their poetry, in fact, is a kind of double-talk, and if we read it in one sense alone we miss a great part of its meaning. For viewed only on the lower level, many of Michelangelo's and Shakespeare's sonnets, for instance, would seem to be inspired by somewhat servile homosexual infatuations, and Herrera's love-poetry, that of a priest for a lady of rank, would appear not only sinful but rather foolish. Since clues to the twofold nature of the poet's subject are not hard to discover even today, when the lower or more literal meaning of love is commonly accepted as the only one, they would certainly not have escaped the Renaissance reader, who had been brought up on the Platonism of the Florentine schools. When Michelangelo addresses Christ and Tomasso Cavalieri, in different poems, with the same words, 'Signor mio', it argues conclusively that what he saw in the young Roman was not merely a handsome person but an incarnation of the divine spirit or, in Eckhart's phrase, a spark of the godhead. By a parallel reasoning, when in our own day W. H. Auden, in an early poem, apostrophizes God as

> Sir, no man's enemy, forgiving all
> But will his negative inversion . . .

it is clear that he is addressing a deity whose attributes are those of a father with psychological insight rather than spiritual majesty. The godhead being beyond all human conceptions, the metaphors in which it is described will vary according to the human virtues which are most highly prized in any age.

Thus Shakespeare, writing in the conventional language of passion to Mr W.H., appears to value his presence as he might a moment of higher consciousness or an entry into the mystical state. How else could the mere memory of this young man compensate him for the misfortune and dereliction which he records in sonnets XXIX and XXX—'When in disgrace with fortune and men's eyes' and 'When to the sessions of sweet silent thought'? The poet's statements appear disproportionate to a generation with different conceptions of love and of divinity. Nevertheless the two levels of meaning undoubtedly coincided for Shakespeare. He did not have to ask himself whether he was speaking directly to Mr W.H. or invoking a state of consciousness in himself that was called up by the sight

or memory of one in whom he glimpsed the divine incarnation.
Sonnet XXXI, though on a lower poetic level than its two
predecessors, begins with the statement that the beloved is
not merely himself but contains within him the spirits of all
those whose absence or loss the poet has mourned in the past:

> Thy bosom is endeared with all hearts,
> Which I by lacking have supposed dead:

and it concludes with an expansion of this thought:

> Thou art the grave where buried love doth live,
> Hung with the trophies of my lovers gone,
> Who all their parts of me to thee did give,
> That due of many now is mine alone:
>   Their images I lov'd I view in thee,
>   And thou—all they—hast all the all of me.

If this sonnet is not addressed to that divine love of which all
human loves are only shadows and reflections, the statement
is not only excessive in its adulation, but patently ridiculous.
It is one thing to say that a new love makes one forget the old,
but quite another to speak of a fresh love for another person as
'the grave where buried love does live': a phrase which
suggests the Resurrection.

An example from Michelangelo will prove the same point.
His sonnet 'Veggio nel tuo bel viso, Signor mio' can yield its
full meaning only if the person to whom it is addressed is seen
in his eternal aspect as a reflection of the Divine. Otherwise,
here too the adulation of the beloved's beauty is so excessive
as to be blasphemously absurd. The last line and a half,
however, so plainly refers to the Saviour as to put the question
beyond all doubt:

> A quel pietoso fonte, onde siam tutti,
> s'assembra ogni beltà che qua si vede,
> più c'altra cosa alle persone accorte;

nè altro saggio abbiam, nè altri frutti
del cielo in terra; chi v'ama con fede
trascende a Dio, e fa dolce la morte.[1]

The Spaniard Herrera too, who addresses his Platonic mistress
by the name of Luz (Light), observes in his third Elegy that her
mere presence transforms the whole of Nature:

Ya son eternas flores los abrojos
i el frio ivierno buelto ya en verano
con la cercana luz de vuestros ojos.[2]

With Herrera, however, the Renaissance convention of
double-talk begins to collapse. He has already advanced
halfway towards the Baroque dissociation of the spiritual and
physical levels. In many respects he was the father of the *culto*
or Latinized manner which was brought to perfection by
Góngora. Though in his beginnings he was the disciple, and
even the imitator, of Garcilaso, the first and greatest poet of
the Spanish Renaissance, his posthumously published collection shows many Baroque characteristics that had not been
present in earlier versions of the same poems, which were
published in his lifetime.[3]

It is the beginning of the Baroque dissociation, however,
between sacred and profane love that is the most surprising
feature in Herrera's poetry. As was suggested above, this
Sevillan priest, who was at the same time an intelligent yet
cantankerous literary theorist, made no pretence that he
enjoyed, or even hoped to enjoy, the profane favours of Doña
Leonor de Córdoba y Aragón, the wife of his friend and patron,
the Conde de Gelves, though he worshipped her under the

---

[1] Everything that is seen here recalls above all else to feeling people
that fount of pity whence we all come; we have no other earnest or fruit of
heaven upon this earth, and he who loves you with faith ascends to God and
accepts death as sweet.
[2] Now the thorns are eternal flowers, and the cold winter is turned to
summer by the proximity of the light of your eyes.
[3] Oreste Macrí, op. cit., pp. 121 et. seq.

name of Luz for more than twenty years. For him she represented the principle of beauty. In using the language of passion,
however, and posing as her rejected lover, Herrera was
undoubtedly expressing, in the same manner as Michelangelo
and Shakespeare but with the beginnings of a Baroque
disproportion, both an aspiration and a consciousness of his
spiritual unworthiness that responded, if not to a factual, at
least to an inner or psychological situation. Nothing in
Herrera's poetry suggests that he had any strong religious
feelings, although a priest. His worship of Luz as the principle
of beauty seems to have stood for him in place of religion.
Mariolatry, in fact, was transformed into the worship of the
'eternal woman', seen in actual incarnation. For his love-
poetry has a depth that is almost entirely absent from his
Canciones, heroic and patriotic odes, which won him admira-
tion in his own day, and which will be considered in a later
chapter.

The patriotic fervour of Herrera's Portuguese contemporary,
Luis de Camões, was far more genuine and deeply rooted. In
contrast to this retiring provincial scholar, Camões was a
soldier and an adventurer, who served his country in her
distant empire and wrote his Virgilian epic, 'Os Lusíadas', on
the subject of her pioneering and christianizing mission. His
love-poems, on the other hand, which were perhaps originally
prompted by an unrequited passion for a princess of the royal
house, speak more clearly even than Herrera's of his inward
condition. Indeed the adoration and fruitless longing that they
express, whatever its origin, show from the beginning strong
marks of subjectivity. We know that, in reality, one of the
greatest sorrows of his life was the loss of his Chinese mistress
in an accident at sea. Such, however, was the Baroque
divorce, already operative in this last poet of the Renaissance,
between reality and the imagination that even more tragic
suffering is expressed in those poems which refer to a situation
that may well have been largely fictitious. What most bitterly
distresses this hard-bitten soldier is not indeed the loss of
any beloved, princess or serving-maid, but his own lack of
feeling:

Passo por meus trabelhos tão isento
de sentimento grande nem pequeno,
que so por la vontade com que peno
me fica Amor devendo mais tormento.[1]

This sonnet suggests that Camões was cut off from the
source of his own emotion, and found in himself a dryness of
the kind frequently described by religious writers, but seldom
in such direct psychological terms. His passion, whether real
or imaginary, is seen in retrospect only. In one of his odes,
indeed, he confesses that the only force which sustains him in
life is memory:

isto só que soubesse, me seria
descanso para a vida que me fica;
co isto afagaria o sofrimento.
    Ah! Senhora, Senhora, que tão rica
estais, que cá tão longe, de alegria,
me sustentais cum doce fingimento!
Em vos afigurando o pensamento,
foge todo o trabalho e toda a pena.
    Só com vossas lembranças
me acho seguro e forte
contra o rosto feroz da fera Morte,
e logo se me ajuntam esperanças
com que a fronte, tornada mais serena,
torna os tormentos graves
em saudades brandas e suaves.[2]

[1] I pass through my ordeals so devoid of grief, great or small, that solely
on account of my willingness to suffer, Love is compelled to inflict more
torment on me.

[2] If only I knew this [that one day she would remember him and pity
him], it would comfort me in my remaining days. With this I would stifle
my grief. Oh, lady, lady, who are so rich in happiness and have been for so
long, support me with a sweet pretence! If I fix my thought on you all my
toil and grief disappear. At the mere thought of you, I find myself secure and
strong against the savage face of fierce death, and then hopes join me with
which henceforward, turned calmer, I may transform severe tortures into
soft and gentle sorrows.

Camões prized the grief with which he responded to his own lack of passion. It was to him a kind of purgative fire. Psychologically more acute than Herrera, he saw at the same time the ideal that he worshipped, and his own state of mind which kept him distant from it. Whereas his epic is rich in the positive values of courage, endurance, and belief in the heroic destiny of his country, his love-poetry expresses a stoicism that is in effect a personal faith. In one of his best-known sonnets he told how the shepherd Jacob, on receiving Leah after serving seven years for Rachel,

> começa de servir outros sete anos,
> dizendo:—Mais servira, se não fora
> para tão longo amor tão curta a vida.[1]

In another sonnet he declared that his fate had never once in his life given him a glimpse of anything he desired[2]; and in yet another[3] he offered to accept all the pains that love might inflict on him in exchange for a single hour of happiness.

Herrera and Camões stand on the threshold of the Baroque, since both in varying degrees speak of a sacred love that has become divorced from any profane or carnal object. The Platonic unity, preached by Castiglione, had completely broken down by the beginning of the seventeenth century. Already John Donne was at times satirizing the carnal from the point of view of the spiritual, and at times the spiritual from the point of view of the carnal. The poem 'Love's Alchymie' rejects all idea of Platonism, and at the same time slights the act of physical possession:

> Our ease, our thrift, our honor, and our day,
> Shall we for this vaine Bubles shadow pay?
>   Ends love in this, that my man,
> Can be as happy, as I can; if he can
> Endure the short scorne of a Bridegroomes play?

---

[1] began to serve another seven years, saying: 'I would serve longer if life were not too short for so long a love.'

[2] No. 46 (ed. Pimpão): 'No mundo quis un tempo que se achasse.'

[3] No. 49 (ed. Pimpão): 'Se, despois de esperança tão perdida.'

That loving wretch that sweares,
'Tis not the bodies marry, but the mindes,
Which he in her Angelique findes,
Would sweare as justly, that he heares,
In that dayes rude hoarse minstralsey, the spheares.
Hope not for minde in women; at their best
Sweetness and wit, they'are but *Mummy*, possest.

Donne was, nevertheless, pre-eminently the poet of the carnal. His thought, part scholastic, part Platonic, part scientific, was frequently that of the disillusioned idealist: a courtier who, having tried Castiglione's method, reports on the reality that he has found. His carnality, however, is not always as cynical as in the lines just quoted. In many poems, indeed, he describes a devotion which, though springing out of physical love and claiming no spiritual overtones, is of itself so strong that he can proclaim in 'The Anniversarie':

All other things to their destruction draw,
Only our love hath no decay;
This no tomorrow hath, no yesterday;
Running it never runs from us away,
But truly keeps his first, last, everlasting day.

Here Donne reaches out to modern conceptions of a sexual love that relies on itself, deriving no sanctions from Platonic idealism or religion.

A previous approach to sexual realism, though still within the framework of the Petrarchan convention, is to be found in the poetry of three women of the Renaissance who proffered both sacred and profane love to a man: in the case of Vittoria Colonna to her husband, in those of Gaspara Stampa and Louise Labé to lovers who rejected them. While celebrating physical passion with a directness that at times rivals Donne's, all nevertheless pay tribute to its transcendental implications. The most revolutionary of the three, Gaspara Stampa, does not narrow her gaze to the 'short scorne of a Bridegroomes play' even when she turns the Platonic convention upside down by preferring the love of Collaltino to that which the holy angels felt in contemplation of the divine presence:

> E come in ciel gran refrigerio e vita
> dal volto Suo solete voi fruire,
> tal io qua giù de la beltà infinita.
>   In questo sol vincete il mio gioire,
> che la vostra è eterna e stabilita,
> e la mia gloria può tosto finire.[1]

In comparing her lot to that of the angels, Gaspara Stampa did not go to the Baroque extreme of accepting the flux of time. She knew that by its impermanence her love was indeed inferior to theirs. It ended quickly, in a disillusioned surrender to 'reason', which took up arms on her behalf and conquered her still unquenched passion:

> E, se non che ragion pur prende l'armi
> e vince il senso, questa acerba cura
> sarebbe or tal che non potrebbe aitarme.[2]

By contrast, Louise Labé is at moments outspokenly sensual, even to the extent of echoing Catullus rather than Petrarch:

> Baise m'encor, rebaise moy et baise:
> Donne m'en un de tes plus savoureux,
> Donne m'en un de tes plus amoureux:
> Je t'en rendrai quatre plus chauds que braise.[3]

Though she may begin one of her sonnets with a stock Petrarchan reference to storms and hail beating against the

[1] And as you are wont to draw great refreshment and life from His face in heaven, so do I here below, from His infinite beauty. In this alone do you surpass my delight, that your glory is eternal, and mine can speedily end.

[2] And if reason did not take up arms and conquer feeling, that bitter care would even now be such that reason could not help me.

[3] Kiss me again, kiss me once more and kiss. Give me one of your most delicious, give me one of your most loving, and I will give you back four hotter than coals.

mountains of Caucasus, she ends with the familiar complaint
of the unsatisfied woman:

> Mais maintenant que tu m'as embrassée,
> Et suis au point auquel tu me voulois,
> Tu as ta flamme en quelque eau arrosée
> Et es plus froid qu'être je ne soulois.[1]

Though she speaks of a passion most foreign to anything
that can be associated with Laura's feelings for Petrarch, Louise
Labé remains generally faithful to the Petrarchan tradition,
even to the extent of repeating its clichés. At moments, too, she
is sufficiently Platonic in sentiment to make use of the commonplaces of the Pythagorean system of thought:

> Voilà du Ciel la puissante harmonie,
> Qui les esprits divins ensemble lie.[2]

Ronsard too, a poet of several loves, saw in each both a
woman and a goddess and, while dwelling on a mistress's
physical charms, was not blind to the impossibility of attaining
complete satisfaction at the worldly level. The treachery of
Time was constantly in his thoughts. He knew that the sole
reality was in heaven even though the heaven he described was
only a French rural landscape populated by nymphs and
shepherds, in which it was always spring. Though he wished
to follow Vergil and Horace, Ronsard remained a Petrarchan
until, under the stress of a passion for a young lady much
above him in station, he wrote the two series of 'Sonnets pour
Hélène', in which he recorded his own middle-aged lack of
charm and her light-hearted intellectual pretensions. In one
sonnet he read her a lecture on them, prophesying that if she
insisted on remaining in the clouds she would fall like Ixion.
For he had now come to recognize the strength of profane love,

---

[1] But now that you have embraced me and I have reached the point that
you wished, you have dowsed your passion with water and are colder than I
was before.

[2] Here is the mighty harmony of Heaven which binds the spirits of the
gods together.

though perhaps only at the moment when he had ceased to enjoy it:

> Bien que l'esprit humain s'enfle par la doctrine
> De Platon, qui le chante influxion des cieux,
> Si est-ce sans le corps qu'il serait ocieux,
> Et aurait beau vanter sa céleste origine.
>
> Par les sens l'âme voit, ell' oit, ell' imagine,
> Ell' a ses actions du corps officieux:
> L'esprit, incorporé, devient ingénieux,
> La matière le rend plus parfait et plus digne.[1]

From this point to that of the sonnets written on his death-bed Ronsard becomes more realistic, and a similar progress can be observed in the poetry of du Bellay between the Petrarchan sonnets of 'L'Olive' and the 'Antiquitéz de Rome'. But his later love-poetry, which is in Latin, is merely a pastiche in the classical manner.

The cleavage between the worldly and transcendental attitudes to love was widened by the court-poet Philippe Desportes, who wrote in the manner of the Pléiade and claimed to be Ronsard's successor. Yet for him poetry was little more than an exercise in a convention that had no necessary connections with facts or events. Reverting to the Petrarchan tradition, he wrote with great accomplishment, adapting most of his poems from the minor poets of Italy, and putting his Muse at the service of other men. For most of his poetry was addressed to ladies at the courts of Henri III and IV on behalf of their lovers, his finest collection, 'Les Amours d'Hippolyte', being commissioned by a nobleman—probably Bussy d'Amboise, who was in love with a princess of the royal blood, the redoubtable Marguerite de Valois.

In the opening sonnet of this sequence Desportes compared

---

[1] Although the human spirit is inflated by the teaching of Plato, who writes that it has flowed down from the heavens, it would be useless without a body, and would boast in vain of its celestial origin. Through the senses the soul sees, hears and thinks. It derives its actions from the busy body. The spirit, given flesh, becomes inventive. Matter makes it more perfect and more worthy.

himself, or rather his patron, to the young Greek Icarus who
flew up to the sun on waxen wings:

> Icare est chu ici, le jeune audacieux,
> Qui pour voler au Ciel eut assez de courage:
> Ici tomba son corps dégarni de plumage,
> Laissant tous braves cœurs de sa chute envieux.[1]

The poem, which is a translation from the Italian of
Sannazzaro, admirably suits the situation of the brave soldier
who aimed at the favours of an exalted princess. The situation
has no relevance to any incident in the poet's life. Yet such was
still the strength of the convention in which he wrote, that the
poem almost succeeds, as do many of his others. The sacred
world of poetry had, in fact, become entirely divorced from the
poet's actual experience.

> Vous volez, comme Icare, en l'air d'un beau malheur,[2]

Ronsard had written to Hélène in the sonnet which follows the
one quoted. Like Icarus, Desportes' poetry soared to the skies
on borrowed wings, and when it fell was found by the merciless
critic François de Malherbe to have no body at all. This first
master of French classicism annotated a copy of Desportes'
works, underlining what he considered the worst passages, and
most unfairly dismissed this court favourite, together with
Ronsard himself, to an oblivion from which he has even now
hardly emerged.

Poetry of this very literary kind was developed along more
original lines by Giambattista Marino, at the court of Louis
XIII, the successor to Desportes' last patron. This master of
artificiality, the model for the French school of Précieux, while
at times given to the composition of elaborate compliments,
was also a poet of profane love. His long, disorderly 'L'Adone'
abounds in scenes of sensual delight.

[1] Icarus fell here, the bold young man, who had the courage to fly to
heaven. Here his body fell stripped of its plumage, leaving all brave hearts
envious of his fall.
[2] Like Icarus, you fly in the air, and a magnificent end awaits you.

> Giovani amanti e donne inamorate,
> in cui ferve d'amor dolce desio,
> per voi scrivo, a voi parlo . . .[1]

he announces at the beginning of canto VIII. Certainly there
is none of Tasso's Renaissance heroism about his stories of gods
and goddesses whose desires are all too human; and the
incidents that he records in many of his sonnets, although
embellished with mythological detail, are clearly based on
experience. Though his ornamental cupids may be of plaster,
his girls are of flesh and blood. The quatrains of his 'Accidente
notturno', for example, are sharply realistic, and the tercets,
though they describe the outcome of his 'adventure by night'
in ironically devious language, are as pleasingly indelicate as
any passage in 'L'Adone':

> L'uscio stridulo apersi, e de la soglia
> fier custode latrante il piè mi morse;
> vigilivan le serve, e 'ntanto sorse
> chiara la luna in ciel più che mai soglia.
>   Velata Lilla mia di bianca spoglia
> le braccia al collo tacita mi porse;
> ma la famiglia garrula vi corse,
> ed io gelai qual gel, tremai qual foglia.
>   I' non so dir se da la luce, accolta
> nel doppio sol de' dolci lumi sui,
> fu lor la vista abbarbagliata e tolta.
>   Coprimmi Amor con l'ali, o forse fui
> cinto da nebbia di sospir sì folta,
> che 'nvisibil divenni agli occhi altrui.[2]

[1] Young lovers and ladies in love, in whom the sweet desire of love
burns, for you I write, to you I speak.

[2] The rasping door opened, the fiercely barking guardian of the
threshold bit my foot. The servants were on the watch, and the moon
immediately came out in the clear sky more brightly than usual. Veiled, my
Lilla with the white body silently put her arms round my neck, but the
talkative servants ran up to her, and I, freezing to death, trembled like a leaf.
I cannot say whether my sight was then dazzled and blinded by the twin
suns of her sweet eyes. Cupid covered me with his wings, or perhaps I was
so wrapped in the thick mist of my sighing that I became invisible to
anyone's eyes.

Marino's poetry is sensual. He is a poet of sight and touch, who seldom reasons. Daphne pursued will turn into a laurel with leaves as fresh and appetizing as the hair of the vanished girl. Kisses are stolen, and excuses offered when the kiss proves cruel: 'Oh!', cries the girl,

> Ahi! tu mordi e non baci,
> tu mi segnasti, ahi! ahi!
> Posso io morir, se più ti bacio mai![1]

The Platonic ideal, the world of classical heroism, the glories of the night-sky—all grow pale as his mistress of the moment rides past in her carriage:

> Non pari a quel, che del mio sole intorno
> per lo cielo d'Amor gira la luce,
> portò già mai vittorïoso duce
> carro superbo in trionfal ritorno,
>   né tale è quel ch'a mezza notte adorno
> d'aurati fregi e candidi riluce;
> né quel ch'a noi da l'orïente adduce
> di chiari lampi incoronato il giorno.[2]

Marino's is a pagan world in which Renaissance poetic values are completely reversed; the earth triumphs over the heavens; and so pervasive is his decorative manner that we even find a Polish Jesuit father, Casimir Sarbiewski, whose Latin poems enjoyed a high reputation throughout the eighteenth century, addressing a young fellow-member of his order in fervently Marinist tones:

> *Lilia manu praefert ALOYSIUS*
> Haec, quae virginiis nituntur lilia culmis,
> Unde verecundas explicuêre comas?

[1] Oh, you are biting, not kissing. You marked me, oh, oh! May I die if ever I kiss you again!

[2] Never did proud chariot carry any victorious general in triumphal procession like this [carriage] which bears the light of my sun around the heavens of Love; nor is that carriage comparable which glistens at midnight [Charles's Wain] trimmed with white and golden ornaments, nor that which day leads from the east, crowned with bright lamps.

Non gererant similes Paestana rosaria flores,
    Nec simili Pharius messe superbat ager.
Non haec purpureis mater Corcyra viretis,
    Nec parit aequoreis pulsa Carystos aquis.
Cum nullas habeant natales lilia terras
    Quis neget e castâ lilia nata manu?[1]

Marino's influence was widespread. Not only French and
Polish, but English and German poets also, adopted his
mannerisms for the writing of complimentary poetry. He was
the father of Preciosity in France, and our Caroline poets,
Richard Crashaw and Thomas Stanley, read and translated
him too. Foreign Marinists, however, imitated the manner
but not the visual qualities of the master's style. His German
disciple, Hofmann von Hofmannswaldau, for example, de-
voting a poem to his mistress's garter, loosed 'in play', is
jocosely sensual. In a poem on another mistress's shoulders he
reviews all the varieties of whiteness, and after discovering that
they are whiter than alabaster, swan's down, or lilies, rather
sententiously concludes that they are a fit resting place for the
gods. Hofmann develops the Marinist conceit to perfection,
but entirely fails to imitate the painter's drawing of flesh and
movement that informs Marino's sonnet on the lady combing
her hair, or the sparkle of the 'Accidente notturno'.

Tristan l'Hermite also, the most faithful disciple of Marino
among the Précieux, lacks his master's power of sustaining a
conceit to the end. Taking a bath in a stream where his
'nymph' Roselie has bathed before him, Tristan finds that the
water has poisoned him; his pangs of love are reawakened:

Je trouve dans ce bain mille pointes de fer,
Et ce qui fut naguère un Ciel pour Roselie,
Dès que j'y suis entré n'est plus rien qu'un Enfer.[2]

[1] Whence have these lilies that are born on virgin stems unfolded their
modest locks? The rose-gardens of Paestum cannot have borne such flowers,
nor did the Egyptian field display such a crop. Mother Corcyra did not bear
them on her crimson lawns, nor yet Carystos [a Black Sea city celebrated for
its marble] beaten by its smooth waters. Since these lilies have no native
soil, who will deny that they sprang from this chaste hand?

[2] I find a thousand iron barbs in this bath, and what was once a heaven
for Roselie, now that I have entered it is nothing but a hell.

Tristan's conclusion drops from Marinism into the tritely
Petrarchan. His protestation of love, moreover, is unconvincing. The loving and sensuous contemplation of a lady
taking a bath is a stock Marinist theme, which Tristan turns
into an idle compliment. Treated by Marino himself, however, in a poem already referred to, or by his disciple, the
young Roman lawyer Marcello Giovanetti in his sonnet 'Bella
ninfa si lavava in un lago', it sustains its brilliant Baroque
hyperbole to the last:

> A l'apparir di lei sopra la sponda,
> al discoprir de gli animati avori,
> al folgorar de l'aurea chioma bionda,
>   alga o scoglio non è, che non s'infiori;
> fiore, che non si specchi entro quell'onda;
> onda, che non sfavilla a tanti ardori.[1]

The Italian Marinists delight in the beauty of women and
are not shy of proclaiming their desire. Though, like their
master, they make play with imagery drawn from the Greek
myths, it is purely ornamental. Though he compares his lovely
silk-spinner to one of the Fates, Bernardo Morando is exact
in his portrayal of her worldly occupation:

> China il sen, nuda il braccio, accesa il volto,
> sottilissime fila Egle traea
> da ricchi vermi, ove bollendo ardea
> breve laghetto in cavo rame accolto.
>   Vago de la sua man, semplice e stolto,
> il mio cor tra quei vermi arder godea,
> e la ruota volubile avvolgea
> lo spirto mio tra quelle sete involto.
>   Ella con l'empia man, ch'ardor non teme,
> nudi rendea fra i gorgoglianti umori
> i bombici di spoglie e me di speme;

---

[1] At her appearance on the bank, at the exposure of her living ivory, at
the glistening of her fair, golden hair, even seaweed or rock would burst into
flower; every flower would reflect itself in the water, and every wave would
sparkle with such heat.

ed agghiacciata il cor fra tanto ardori
bella Parca d'amor, filava insieme
ricche spoglie e le membra e lacci ai cori.[1]

The pictorial and the profane preside together over the large output of Marino's Italian followers, who continued to develop his themes and follow his style until the end of the century, by which time it appeared somewhat provincial. For the revulsion against Baroque, which began in France, had by then spread to Italy, and though it stimulated no new poetry, had destroyed the reputation of the old. From this loss of favour the Marinists have not even yet recovered. The appraisals of Benedetto Croce, who early in this century introduced a two-volume collection of Marino's lyrics and an anthology of his followers, were at best patronizing and at worst hostile. To him both the 'sensuality' and the 'ingenuity' of these seventeenth-century poets were qualities to be condemned. A more recent critic, Giuseppe Guido Ferrero, while setting out to be more generous, concludes the introduction to his excellent anthology, *Marino e i Marinisti*, with the judgement that 'the revolution undertaken by our Baroque versifiers failed, on account of an indisputable lack of creative genius, and also because of the poets' lack of *commitment*'. Ferrero refuses to arraign them in the manner of some of his predecessors for failing to devote their poetry to the service of an ideal, whether ethical, religious, or political, but accuses them of having insufficient faith in their task as innovators.

An equally severe examination of the French, German, or Spanish poets of the time might reach an equally damaging conclusion. None of them was committed to any cause, and none was endowed with the major creative power of the great Renaissance poets, Tasso, Spenser, Camões, or their successor

[1] Her breast bent, her arm bare, her face flushed, Aigle was drawing a subtle thread from rich worms where a little pool was boiling, contained in a copper pot. Attracted by her simple, foolish hand, my heart was delighted to grow hot with those worms, and her fickle wheel spun my spirit round after that drawn silk. She with her pitiless hand, that feared no heat, stripped the worms naked in the seething liquid and gave me hope; and with heart frozen by all this heat, this beauteous Fate of love spun at the same time rich clothes for limbs and toils for hearts.

Milton. Fortunately, however, French, German, and Spanish critics have judged Baroque poetry by its own standards, which were defined long ago by Wölfflin in relation to the art of painting:

> The general tendency [of Baroque] is to produce the picture no longer as a self-existing piece of the world, but as a passing show, which the spectator may enjoy only for a moment. The final question is not one of full-face or profile, vertical or horizontal, tectonic or a-tectonic, but whether the figure, the total picture as a visible form, looks intentional or not.[1]

The sensuous vision of the Marinists is certainly 'intentional'. In a world of failing beliefs and growing rigidity of thought they seized on a visual impression and elaborated it by use of the sustained conceit. Compared with that of the English Baroque poet, John Donne, their intellectual range was extremely narrow. Marino's poetry is 'the very opposite of a revelation of the soul'.[2]

By developing situations known and accepted in the circle he was addressing, however, the poet of 'L'Adone', with consummate ingenuity and no aid from transcendentalism, greatly extended the richness of that circle's immediate sensual apprehension.[3]

[1] Wölfflin, op. cit., p. 126.
[2] Rudolf Stamm, op. cit., p. 281. (Roedel, *Die Italienische Barockdichtung*)
[3] Rousset, op. cit., pp. 241–2.

4

A stately pleasure-dome

'IT WOULD seem to the Baroque a sin against life', wrote Wölfflin, 'if sculpture were to settle into a definite plane. It does not look to one side only but possesses a much greater area of radiation.'[1]

It is possible to think of Morando's sonnet on the beautiful silk-spinner or Marino's 'Bella sonatrice', with its elaborate comparison between the fair musician's ebony and ivory bows (her brow and her hand):

> Duo archi adopra e con duo archi offende
> questa ch'arciera e Musa il mondo ammira:
> un con la bella man ne move e tira,
> un nel ciglio seren ne curva e tende
> D'ebeno l'un, l'altro d'avorio splende,[2]

as portraits or sculptures that have still a single subject, treated on a single plane. But already in 'Accidente notturno' and 'Madonna in carrozza' the 'area of radiation' has widened. The former moves from realism into metaphor, the latter even further, from the sight of a lady in a carriage to contemplation of the sun, the stars, and the miraculous assumption of the prophet Elijah. Both sonnets appear to contain an explosive charge which makes for a sudden and violent expansion of

---

[1] Op. cit., p. 108.

[2] She uses two bows, and wounds with two bows, she whom the world admires as archer and Muse: one she moves to and fro with her fair hand, the other she curves and straightens on her calm brow. One shines like ebony, the other like ivory.

interest. Perhaps it is the poet's spiritual unease, which would have been expressed directly in a Protestant country, that drives him to the excitable violence of his imagery. Certainly it is in the Catholic countries that the conceit flourished most vigorously, not merely enhancing the detail of the poem as it did for Donne, but developing to the point where, as in 'Madonna in carrozza', the whole statement is made by imagery.

Marino does not, however, represent the extreme of this Baroque style. His 'L'Adone', though overweighed by sensuous digressions, still takes the form of a narrative poem in the manner of Tasso's 'Gerusalemme liberata'. It is the Spaniard, Luis de Góngora, in a country where freedom of thought and comment was even more restricted than in Italy or at the court of Louis XIII, who carried the *culto* style to its furthest limits in his 'Soledades'. The values of this long poem, the second part of which was left unfinished, are those of an extended lyric rather than an epic. Though ostensibly telling the story of a handsome young sailor shipwrecked on an island of fisherfolk and goatherds, it in fact pays little attention to narrative. All its statements are oblique, and even a Spaniard can hardly capture its full meaning without a prose translation which takes into account the several ambiguities that are contained in every line.[1] Manner triumphs over matter throughout the poem, and there is little human feeling or comment on life. The poet, a disappointed man who harboured many grudges and devoted much of his life to the pursuit of a pension which he never succeeded in obtaining, conceals himself almost completely behind his artifices. Unlike Marino, he does not, as I have said, indulge in digressions. His poem is, however, always at one remove from his ostensible subject. 'Las Soledades' is a painter's commentary on a story which is not told but obliquely hinted at. The reader is left to work out the equivalence between Góngora's images and the natural objects which they represent. When the sailor meets six shepherd-girls on the island their singing and dancing,

[1] See Luis de Góngora, 'Las Soledades', con versión en prosa de Dámaso Alonso.

movement and colour, are made to serve the purpose of realistic description. What we see are not the girls but the formalized movement of shapes and colours which suggest objects, some of which must be taken for real, but most of which are mere visual associations.

> Otra con ella montaraz zagala
> juntaba el cristal líquido al humano
> por el arcaduz bello de una mano
> que al uno menosprecia, al otro iguala.

> Del verde margen otra las mejores
> rosas traslada y lilios al cabello,
> o por lo matizado o por lo bello,
> si Aurora no con rayos, Sol con flores.

> Negras pizarras entre blancos dedos
> ingeniosa hiere otra, que dudo
> que aun los peñascos la escucharan quedos.
>   Al son pues deste rudo
>   sonoroso instrumento
>   —lasciva el movimento,
>   mas los ojos honesta—
> altera otra, bailando, la floresta.[1]

> ('Soledad' 1, lines 243–58)

[1] With this girl there was another shepherdess of these mountains, who was washing her face in [or perhaps *drinking* from] the water of this spring, so that she united the liquid crystal of the water with the human crystal of her face by way of the lovely conduit of her hand, which equalled the crystal of her face in beauty and surpassed the crystal of the water.

Another shepherdess is putting the finest roses and lilies of the green bank in her hair, which is in its many tints like the dawn with its rays, and made up in its beauty like the sun on flowers [that is to say made up of flowers, the attributes of the dawn, and rays, the attributes of the sun]. Another dexterously bruises black stones between her white fingers with such skill that I doubt whether the rocks themselves [a reference to Orpheus] could have stayed still if they had heard her. To the music of this sweet and rough instrument, another shepherdess, with wanton movements but a modest expression, arouses and disturbs the thicket [and its inhabitants] with her dance. (Translation based on prose paraphrase in Dámaso Alonso, op. cit.)

The world has been conjured away in favour of an
Arcadia, which is itself in dissolution. Girls turn into flowers,
their hands are crystal conduits that convey water to their
mouths or faces, and their bucolic music reminds the poet of
Orpheus charming the rocks. The world of reality has in fact
yielded to a substitute world of art, in which all natural
objects shrink into their formal equivalents, and the eye with
its swift evaluation of resemblances and contrasts usurps the
functions of the poet's mind, which could not exercise itself
freely in a land where theological conformity was exacted to
the last detail.

Even the world of art, moreover, or the unnamed island on
which the sailor landed to escape the ocean, is itself in the
process of dissolution. The old goatherd who takes him a tour
of its sights points out the ruins of what was an ancient city in
the days when he himself wore a captain's armour. We have
here a possible reference to Æneas's view of the destruction of
Troy. The captain speaks, but is interrupted by the wild
onrush of a wolf-hunt, which sweeps the old man away
with it:

> 'Aquellas que los árboles apenas
> dejan ser torres hoy—dijo el cabrero
> con muestras de dolor extraordinarias—
> las estrellas nocturnas luminarias
>   eran de sus almenas,
> cuando el que ves sayal fué limpio acero.
> Yacen ahora, y sus desnudas piedras
>   visten piadosas yedras:
>   que a rüinas ya a estragos,
> sabe el tiempo hacer verdes halagos.'
>
> Con gusto el joven y atención le oía,
> cuando torrente de armas y de perros,
> que si precipitados no los cerros,
> las personas tras de un lobo traía,
> tierno discurso y dulce compañía
>   dejar hizo al serrano,

> que—del sublime espacioso llano
> al huésped al camino reduciendo—
>   al venatorio estruendo,
>   pasos dando veloces,
> número crece y multiplica voces.[1]

Góngora has shown the island pageantry as for ever in movement. Gazing after the old man, the sailor sees in him a contradictory blending of the gods Pan and Mars, an armed Pan or a Mars who was half a goat:

> Armado a Pan o semicapro a Marte.

But his reflections are interrupted by the sound of a girl singing beside a spring. All is in turmoil, everything passes, and Nature covers the ruins of this one-time island Troy with the piteous fingers of the ivy. The poem flows, but is so strictly constructed, so unified by the music of its language and the strange Latinate inversions of its phrases, that it seems to offer a greater permanency than its legend.

The strictest poetic forms often call out the highest inventive qualities. Such a poet as Marino expresses himself perfectly in the sonnet but when writing in loose unrhymed measures allows sound to dictate sense. So also the mental restrictions under which Góngora and his generation were compelled to work stimulated them to a more concentrated

---

[1] 'These towers, today almost hidden by the trees, were once so tall that the stars seemed to be night-lamps on their battlements. And this was when I wore a warrior's bright armour instead of the shepherd's coat. Now the towers are overthrown, and the piteous ivy covers their naked feet. For just as time knows how to mitigate disasters, so it knows how to cover ruins with flattering greenery.' The young man was listening to the goatherd with delighted attention, when a troop of huntsmen, chasing a wolf with arms and dogs (so headlong a troop that it was more like a torrent dragging people, or even the crags themselves, in its wake), made the countryman interrupt the touching story he was telling and the gracious company in which he stood. So guiding his guest back from the great high look-out to the road, he quickly turned to the noisy crowd of huntsmen, adding himself to their numbers and his voice to their clamour. (Translation adapted from Alonso, op. cit.)

virtuosity than was achieved by their contemporaries, the French *libertins*, Saint-Amant, Théophile de Viau, and others, who were comparatively free to express their heretical notions, though de Viau's eccentric Platonism finally led him into trouble.

Góngora used the method of the 'Soledades' in a variety of poems of far simpler form. A short piece in the traditional metre of the *romance* (or historical ballad) tells of some country-girls—sisters to those encountered by his shipwrecked sailor —whom the poet discovered in the pinewoods of Júcar. They too bruised black stones (which represent their castanets) between their white fingers—an ivory instrument which the Muses would envy—and compelled the birds, the flowing stream, and the leaves to be silent, in order not to disturb their song. It is remarkable that the poet can adapt the direct and unsophisticated measure of the ballad to such artificial ends as those of the poem's last lines:

> Entre rama y rama
> cuando el ciego dios
> pide al sol los ojos
> por verlas mejor,
> los ojos del Sol
> la veréis pisar,
> *unas por piñones*
> *otras por bailar.*[1]

Góngora paints his scene allusively. Marino, comparing a girl's hand or comb to an ivory boat cleaving the golden waves of her hair, develops his metaphor, and extends it to the length of his sonnet. Quevedo, whose sonnet on a similar theme we have compared with Marino's, describes three aspects of his mistress's hair, its waviness, its colour, and its resilience beneath the comb, in his opening line. But Góngora's habit is

---

[1] Between the branches, when the blind god [Cupid] begs the sun for his eyes to see them better, you will see them treading on the eyes of the sun [the patches of sunlight between the trees], some for pine-nuts, others for dancing's sake.

to leap one or more stages in his chain of similes, and leave his reader to deduce that when he writes 'Los ojos del sol' he is describing round patches of sunlight on the ground that have the shape of eyes, and that also represent the sun's powers of vision, since only where his rays fall can the sun see. Góngora's 'painterly' method is like that of the Impressionists; patches of juxtaposed colour are made to suggest objects, which are not outlined but bathed in light. An interesting comparison can be made between his poetry and the painting of Velázquez who in his Roman garden-pieces in the Prado was feeling for a similar method, which he brought to perfection thirty years after Góngora's death, in his final portraits and in the superbly artificial composition of his court picture, 'Las Meninas'. Its double mirror reflection, while removing the spectator by two degrees from the real scene, re-creates it for him in greater fulness by this seemingly simple trick than would have been possible by direct portrayal.

The complete portrayal at which Góngora aimed was less realistic. The world that he describes is a highly coloured illusion. For him all things are appearances which can be reduced to their primal qualities. Snow is a symbol for everything that is white. *Woven snow* ('nieve hilada') consequently stands for white linen tablecloths, *flowing snow* ('volante nieve') for the white feathers of a bird, *snow clad in a thousand colours* ('nieve de colores mil vestida') denotes the limbs of peasant girls in their bright dresses, and, at farthest remove from a natural description, *fragrant cups that May has snowed to the ground* must be translated as scented white lilies that have grown in spring. In this extreme of the impressionistic style the visual associations are always made to stand for reality. Crystal *is* water; gold *is* a girl's hair, or honey, or olive oil, or ripened wheat.[1] The world is conventionalized. Nature is the starting-point, but it is quickly abandoned in favour of a pictorial or literary idea. The method is, as Dámaso Alonso suggests, the end-product of an evolution which begins in the Greek pastoral and completes itself in the Italian Renaissance.[2]

[1] See Dámaso Alonso, '*Estudios y ensayos gongorinos*', pp. 72–3.
[2] Op. cit., p. 71.

Certainly, despite its allusiveness, it preserves its affinities with pastoral. Góngora's 'Fábula de Polifemo y Galatea', his most important poem after the 'Soledades', follows a favourite Renaissance theme, which owed its popularity first in Italy and then in Spain to its treatment in the 'Metamorphoses' of Ovid. Marino had devoted a series of sonnets to it, and narrated the loves of Acis and Galatea in canto XIX of 'L'Adone'. But whereas earlier poets made much of Polyphemus' love-song to the unfeeling and frightened Galatea, whose heart was given to the youthful Acis, Góngora's prime interest is the Baroque contrast between Galatea's beauty and Polyphemus' hatred of Acis; between the beauty of Sicily and the arid rocky scenery of the monster's yawning cave.

> De este, pues, formidable de la tierra
> bostezo, el melancólico vacío
> a Polifemo, horror de aquella sierra,
> bárbara choza es, albergue umbrío
> y redil espacioso donde encierra
> cuanto las cumbres ásperas cabrío,
> de los montes esconde: copia bella
> que un silbo junta y un peñasco sella.[1]

In contrast Galatea is created of brightness and colour, a creature of another world:

> Purpúreas rosas sobre Galatea
> la Alba entre lilios cándidos deshoja:
> duda el Amor cuál mas su color sea,
> o púrpura nevada, o nieve roja.
> De su frente la perla es, eritrea,

---

[1] The melancholy hollow of this enormous yawn in the earth served the giant Polyphemus, the terror of those mountains, as a rough cabin, dark shelter, and vast pen in which he shut his herd of goats which was so great as to cover the rough peaks of the mountains: a numerous herd that was summoned by a whistle and sealed into the cave with a rock.

émula vana. El ciego dios se enoja
y, condenado su esplendor, la deja
pender en oro al nácar de su oreja.[1]

Whereas 'Polifemo' exploits the contrast between the beautiful and the monstrous,[2] Góngora's romance 'Angélica y Medoro', which is founded on an incident in Ariosto's 'Orlando Furioso', provides a picture of love in modest retirement that is anti-heroic and highly decorative. The marriage bed of the little Moor, who has escaped from battle, and the beloved of Orlando, who gladly gives herself to him, is described in mock-Martial terms:

> Todo es gala el Africano,
> su vestido espira olores,
> el lunado arco suspende,
> y el corvo alfanje depone.
> Tórtolas enamoradas
> son sus roncos atambores,
> y los volantes de Venus
> sus bien seguidos pendones
> Desnuda el pecho anda ella,
> vuela el cabello sin orden;
> si le abrocha, es con claveles,
> con jazmines si le coge.[3]

The pastoral and the heroic poem are thus presented afresh by means of Góngora's oblique vision. The story no longer moves directly forward; it is no longer confined to one

---

[1] Dawn has shed the petals of deep red roses among pure white lilies [her pink cheeks and white skin] on Galatea. Cupid is in doubt whether her complexion is snowy purple or pink snow. The Red Sea pearl competes in vain with her brow. The blind god is enraged by the pearl's effrontery and, proclaiming its splendour inferior, leaves it to hang on the mother-of-pearl of her ear, set in the gold of an earring.

[2] See Dámaso Alonso, *Góngora y el 'Polifemo'*, pp. 208–13.

[3] The African is all gallantry, his clothes give off sweet odours. He hangs up his crescent bow and takes off his curved scimitar. Enamoured turtle-doves are his hoarse drums, and the birds of Venus his well-followed banners. She goes with naked breast, her hair flying in disorder; if she pins it up, it is with carnations; if she ties it, it is with jasmine.

plane. The 'area of radiation' has been extended by the use of ironic contrast and by indulgence in decorative effects, which serve the purpose of removing the action out of the world of reality into the 'pleasure dome' of pure art. In this Góngora stands at the end of a line of development that had begun in the Renaissance. 'The Greco-Latin world picture', wrote Dámaso Alonso, 'had reduced all the forms and activities of life to a series of archetypes . . . Mythology, in its broadest and primary sense, transforms the abstract into concrete symbols. Love is reduced to the boy, Cupid; war to Mars; music and its powers to Orpheus or Amphion; swiftness to Atalanta . . . etc.' The Renaissance revived these symbols. 'For a Renaissance writer', continues Alonso, 'every object had its place in the world-order, and belonged to a given point in a fixed system. All the phenomena of reality could thus be defined by their mythological constellations.'[1] The relation between this convention and that of spiritual Platonism was a close one. In both cases any terrestrial event was seen to conform to a mythical or ideological 'idea' or 'type'. This was a principal of Biblical exposition also, which survived long enough to lead Pascal, in his *Pensées*, into drawing some very strange analogies. By Góngora's time, however, Greco-Latin and even at times Christian myths had come to be used decoratively, and for their own sake. They formed a body of generally accepted imagery, such as we do not possess today, when there is no agreed body of reference common to the poet and his reader. It was indeed in an attempt to remedy this that W. B. Yeats elaborated a new cosmological theory in his prose 'Vision', and Robert Graves compiled his compendium of myth in 'The White Goddess'.

The contemporaries of Góngora, in Spain and also in Italy, retold their favourite legends of Hero and Leander, Pyramus and Thisbe, Daphne and Apollo, Orpheus and Eurydice and the Rape of Europa, drawing principally on Ovid for their stories, but elaborating them in many ways that were essentially pictorial. Thus the frieze of their 'pleasure-dome' was liberally ornamented with subjects taken from the

[1] Op. cit., p. 128.

past, but rendered with a chiaroscuro that sometimes looks forward to that of the Romantics. The 'Orfeo' of Juan de Jáuregui, for example, a critic and imitator of Góngora, presents a lurid landscape in the manner of Salvator Rosa, and places in it that entrance to the underworld through which Orpheus must journey in search of his lost wife:

> De ciegas ondas lago ponzoñoso
> bate en la peña y riega su boscaje,
> que al basilisco, y aspid venenoso
> aun fuera su licor mortal brevaje:
> humos exala, que en el viento ocioso
> no otorgan a las aves hospedaje,
> y ellas buscan, huyendo el vapor ciego,
> antes arder en la región del fuego.
>
> Nunca por yerro de accidente en esta
> palude, o risco, o selva retegida,
> vil pece, tosca fiera, ave funesta,
> gruta, o cueva recoge, arbol anida,
> el denso evaporar el aire infesta;
> toda la estancia es odio de la vida,
> y en su distrito con silencio advierte
> que se origina el reino de la muerte.[1]

Though Jáuregui raises a shiver of Romantic apprehension, his hellish landscape—which owes something to passages in Lucan's 'Pharsalia', of which he made an admirable translation—is less disturbing than Polyphemus' cave as it is described in Góngora's poem. For Jáuregui was an intellectual poet, who attained his effects by conscious art; Góngora, on the other hand, was driven to excesses of hyperbole by an

[1] A poisonous lake of blind waters washes the rocks and irrigates the thicket, the waters of which would be fatal to the basilisk and the poisonous snake. From it rise fogs on a heavy wind that drives away the birds who, flying from the thick vapours, prefer to burn in the fiery regions. Never by any chance does a humble fish, wild beast or bird of prey seek a hole, cave or tree for nesting in this swamp, or rock or tangled thicket. The dense exhalations hang on the air; the whole site is abominated by life, and issues a silent warning that in its neighbourhood begins the kingdom of the dead.

emotional unrest that he could not express directly. The contrast between the monster and the maiden had a greater psychological relevance for him than the tale of Orpheus for Jáuregui who brought it to a happy ending. The 'absolute disorder' of Góngora's stanza, with which he concludes his description of the one-eyed monster's den, reminds Dámaso Alonso of the scene of an earthquake.[1] All the words have been shaken out of their natural order. Those of Jáuregui, on the other hand, are neatly grouped in triplets, after the *culto* manner, which derived from Herrera and which the poet practised here in a far more concentrated fashion than in his somewhat more direct lyrical poetry. The same technique could, however, be used to paint a landscape of peace, as it was by Góngora's contemporary, Pedro Espinosa, a poet of small output who spent part of his life as a religious hermit. Espinosa's 'Fábula del Genil' tells of the love of the god of that small river, which flows beneath the walls of Granada, for the nymph Cynaris, who, given to him in reluctant marriage, breaks into tears and dissolves in water. The description of the underwater palace of the river-god Betis, the classical name for the Guadalquivir, and the Genil's speech in praise of the flowers that grow on his banks, gently blend the natural and mythical in a picture as idyllic as Jáuregui's and Góngora's are agitated.

> Vestida está mi margen de espadaña
> y de viciosos apios y mastranto,
> y el agua clara, como el ámbar, baña
> troncos de mirtos y de lauro santo;
> no hay en mi margen silbadora caña,
> ni adelfa; mas violetas y amaranto,
> de donde llevan flores en las faldas
> para hacer las Hénides guirnaldas.
>
> Hay blandos lirios, verdes mirabeles,
> y azules guarnecidos alhelíes;
> y allí las clavellinas y claveles
> parecen sementera de rubíes;

[1] See *Poesía española, ensayo de métodos y limites estilísticos*, p. 354.

D

hay ricas alcatifas, y alquiceles
rojos, blancos, gualdados y turquíes,
y derraman las auras con su aliento
ámbares y azahares por el viento.[1]

The decorations of the palace of art were varied. But few
Spanish Baroque poems displayed originality of subject,
thought, or social standpoint. Like the Marinisti, the Gón-
gorists strove above all for originality of treatment. Thus a
sonnet by one of Góngora's followers, Gabriel Bocángel, 'On
hearing a trumpet sounded at nightfall by a convict over the
sea', creates a striking synaesthesia, or confusion of the senses,
that forestalls Rimbaud's, and, while pointing the most
commonplace of morals, paints a scene that no Renaissance
poet would have attempted:

Ya falta el Sol; que quieto el mar, y el cielo,
niegan unidos la distante arena:
un ave metal el aire estrena,
que vuela en voz, quanto se niega en vuelo.
Hijo infeliz del Africano suelo
es, que hurtado al rigor de la cadena,
hoy música traición hace a su pena
(si pena puede haber donde hay consuelo).
Suene tu voz (menos que yo) forzado,
pues tu clarín es sucesor del remo,
y alternas el gemido con el canto.
Mientras yo al mar de Venus condenado,
de un extremo de amor paso a otro extremo,
y porque alivia, aun se me niega el llanto.[2]

[1] My bank is clothed with reed-mace and luxuriant wild celery and
mint, and the water, clear as amber, bathes the trunks of myrtles and sacred
laurel; there is no whistling reed or bay on my banks, but violets and
amaranth, from which they take flowers in their skirts to make garlands
for the nymphs of Genil. There are gentle lilies, green crowsfoot,
purple-edged stocks, and there the pinks and carnations seem a crop of
rubies. There are fine carpets and red, white and yellow and blue tablecloths, and the breezes spill with their breath amber and orange-blossom
down the wind.

[2] Now the sun is missing, and quietly the sea and the sky together deny
[the existence of] the distant beach; a metal bird opens its first track through

The picture is clear. Even the trumpet sound that flies like a bird almost takes visible shape in Bocángel's paradoxical description. It is in the final tercet that the poem fails. The middle-aged librarian of Granada, who conjures with concepts in so learned a style, cannot command a modern reader's belief that he suffers worse tortures through love than the galley-slave at his oar. Baroque excess has defeated itself. The 'area of radiation' has narrowed to the breadth of the poet's ingenuity.

At the end of the Baroque epoch, and in the New World, a final attempt to use the Gongorist method in an intellectual instead of a visual way triumphantly succeeded. The Mexican poet Juana Inés de la Cruz openly proclaimed her poem 'El sueño' an imitation of 'Las Soledades'. Like Góngora's masterpiece, it requires a prose expansion and elucidation if it is to be fully understood. The Mexican poet's vision is, however, all-embracing. Far from elaborating a single legend, she takes the whole cosmos for her subject. Her vision in the series of dreams that form the subject of 'El sueño' reaches to the peaks of the mountains and the depths of the ocean. In sleep she is tempted by the possibility of attaining universal knowledge; she glimpses the 'universal categories' of Aristotle, and touches on the Christocentric system of Duns Scotus. Though the poem's manner is Gongoristic, its subject recalls that of Lucretius, or the last cantos of the 'Paradiso', and looks forward to 'Le Cimetière marin' of Valéry and the 'Muerte sin fin' of the modern Mexican poet, José Gorostiza. A woman of great and precocious learning, Juana de la Cruz wrote love-poetry, religious verses, and plays while serving the wife of the Mexican viceroy as lady-in-waiting. After losing her lover she became a nun but continued to read widely and frequent intelligent society. In biting prose she defended her right to

the sky, flying as a voice, though it denies itself [i.e. is invisible] in its flight. It is an unhappy son of the African soil who, stealing from the harshness of his chain, is committing musical treachery to his sorrow (if sorrow can exist where there is consolation). Sound your voice under restraint (but less so than I), since your trumpet has succeeded your oar, and you have interrupted your groans with its song. Whilst I, a galley-slave on Venus' sea, pass from one extreme of love to another, and tears, since they relieve me, are denied.

read what she would against the attacks of timid and narrow-minded clerics. The atmosphere of Mexico was, fortunately, more favourable to unconventional thought than metropolitan Spain; and 'El sueño' is certainly bolder than anything that has been written in the Peninsula since the suppression of Erasmist thought in the reign of Philip II. Yet though she attempted to resolve the meaning of the cosmos in purely philosophical terms, she was forced in the end to fall back on theology. In its bare thousand lines, however, 'El sueño' moves from a picturesque and historical allusiveness to a concentrated bareness of statement that passes beyond the age of Góngora into the century of his admirer, Stéphane Mallarmé.

There is great variation of light and shade, if not of colour, in the poem's introductory description of the sinister creatures that wake as night descends on the world:

> Con tardo vuelo y canto, del oído
> mal, y aun peor del ánimo admitido,
> la avergonzada Nictimene acecha
> de las sagradas puertas los resquicios,
> o de las claraboyas eminentes
> los huecos más propicios
> que capaz a su intento le abren brecha,
> y sacrílega llega a los lucientes
> faroles sacros de perenne llama,
> que extingue, si no infama,
> en licor claro la materia crasa
> consumiendo, que el árbol de Minerva
> de su fruto, de prensas agravado,
> congojoso sudó y rindió forzado.[1]

[1] With slow flight and song—disquieting to the ear and even more so to the mind—the shameful Nictimene [the owl. Once a maiden of Lesbos, she has been changed into a bird as punishment for a shameful crime] watches the chinks of the temple doors, or the holes in its high skylights that may afford her a suitable entry; and once in, she goes sacrilegiously to the sacred lamps of perpetual flame, which she either puts out or treats with greater irreverence, drinking their oil: raw material or grease supplied by Minerva's tree [the olive] in the form of an anxious sweat or forced tribute extracted from its fruit by the weight of the press. (Translation based on prose version of Alfonso Méndez Plancarte.)

The dream of the cosmos, however, which forms the second stage of the Vision, is naturally less picturesque. It takes the form of a hymn to the powers of the human mind, seen in the form of the ever-watchful eagle:

De Júpiter el ave generosa
—como al fin Reina—por no darse entera
al descanso, que vicio considera
si de preciso pasa, cuidadosa
de no incurir de omisa en el exceso,
a un solo pie librada fía el peso
y en otro guarda el cálculo pequeño
—despertador reloj del leve sueño—,
porque, si necesario fué admitido,
no pueda dilatarse continuado,
antes interrumpido
del regio sea pastoral cuidado.
¡Oh de la Majestad pensión gravosa,
que aun el menor descuido no perdona!
Causa, quizá, que ha hecho misteriosa,
circular, denotando, la corona,
en círculo dorado,
que el afan es no menos continuado.
    El sueño todo, en fin, lo poseía;
todo, en fin, el silencio lo ocupaba:
aun el ladrón dormía;
aun el amante no se desvelaba.[1]

[1] The noble bird of Jupiter, who considers that, as king [in Spanish, queen] of the birds, he should not give himself entirely to repose, since it would be wrong to sleep more than is necessary, takes care to commit no sins of omission. Therefore, resting his entire weight on one claw, he holds a small stone in the other—an alarm clock in case he dozes. So even if he cannot help falling asleep for a moment, it will not be for long, and his royal duty of watching his flock will wake him. How heavy is the weight of Majesty, which will not allow a careless moment! This is perhaps the reason why the crown has been made round, to denote by its continuous golden circle that the king's watchfulness must be continuous also.
Sleep had now finally mastered all things, silence pervaded everything; even thieves were sleeping, even lovers no longer stayed awake. (Translation based on Plancarte's.)

Juana de la Cruz confessed that this was the only one of her poems that she had written for her own pleasure. Nevertheless it found few admirers for two hundred and fifty years. Only latterly, with the revised enthusiasm for Góngora and the growth of interest in the Mexican cultural tradition, has her reputation been rehabilitated, first on account of her sonnets and carols, and secondly for this remarkable poem, the character of which is so strongly Mexican. Bold statement and the intellectual treatment of abstruse themes are peculiarly characteristic of the Mexican Baroque.

Luis de Sandoval y Zapata, for example, one among the many seventeenth-century poets of New Spain (the name by which the present republic was then known), addressed one of the best of his sonnets, which lie for the most part unpublished in the National Library of Mexico, to the Aristotelian 'Materia prima', surely the most abstract subject that a poet could choose:

> Materia que de vida te informaste,
> en cuántas metamórfosis viviste?
> Ampo oloroso en el jazmín te viste,
> y en la ceniza pálida duraste.
>
> Después que tanto horror te desnudaste,
> rey de las flores púrpura vestiste.
> En tantas muertas formas, no moriste:
> tu sér junto a la muerte eternizaste.
>
> ¿ Qué discursiva luz nunca despiertes,
> y no mueras al ímpetu invisible
> de las aladas horas, homicida?
>
> ¿ Qué, no eres sabia junto a tantas muertes?
> ¿ Qué eres, naturaleza incorruptible
> habiendo estado viuda a tanta vida?[1]

[1] Material that informed yourself with life, in how many metamorphoses have you lived? You saw yourself a sweet-smelling snowflake in the jasmine, and lived on in its pale dust. After you stripped yourself of this horror, you put on purple as king of the flowers. In so many dead forms, yet you did not die; you eternalized your being in the neighbourhood of death. Which of light's multiple forms do you not awaken, and why do you not succumb to the invisible and murderous attack of the winged hours? Why are you not wise after so many deaths? What are you, incorrupt nature, having been widowed of so much life?

The many-coloured dome has been reduced to its vast skeleton of primal matter. The gaudy pageant of the picturesque in the end failed to deceive the poets. What was once snowflake, jasmine, and finally dust, has survived death but is now reduced to nothing. Góngora had reached the same conclusion in one of his earliest sonnets which, despite a concentration of colour that is absent from the Mexican poem, is ultimately no less despairing:

> Mientras por competir con tu cabello,
> oro bruñido, el Sol relumbra en vano,
> mientras con menosprecio en medio el llano
> mira tu blanca frente el lilio bello;
>   mientras a cada labio, por cogello,
> siguen más ojos que al clavel temprano,
> y mientras triunfa con desdén lozano
> del luciente cristal tu gentil cuello;
>   goza cuello, cabello, labio y frente,
> antes que lo que fué en tu edad dorada
> oro, lilio, clavel, cristal luciente,
>   no sólo en plata o víola troncada
> se vuelva, mas tú y ello juntamente
> en tierra, en humo, en polvo, en sombra, en nada.[1]

Compared with the many Renaissance poems on the theme of 'Gather ye rosebuds', Góngora's sonnet dwells not on the pleasures to be plucked by the bold lover, but on their transitoriness. Like Marvell, he reminds his mistress, even as he woos her, that

> Thy Beauty shall no more be found;
> Nor, in thy marble Vault, shall sound
> My echoing Song . . .

[1] While, in competition with your hair, the sun, like burnished gold, gleams in vain, while your white forehead despises the lovely lily in the midst of the plain, while more eyes follow each lip, to catch it, than follow the early carnation, and while your gentle neck triumphs with proud disdain over the lucent crystal, enjoy neck, hair, lip and forehead, before what was in your golden age gold, lily, carnation and lucent crystal not only turns to silver or plucked violet, but you and it together become earth, smoke, dust, shadow, nothing.

but does not even trouble to invite her to play. Nor does he reproach the lady like Hofmann von Hofmannswaldau, who, after reminding her,

> Es wird der bleiche Tod mit seiner kalten Hand
> Dir endlich mit der Zeit um deine Brüste streichen,[1]

tells her that her heart alone has power to live on since it is made of adamant:

> Dein Herze kann allein zu aller Zeit bestehen,
> Dieweil es die Natur aus Diamant gemacht.

Marvell and Hofmann, while ever conscious that

> yonder all before us lie
> Desarts of vast Eternity,

leave some room for pleasure in the world of Time; Góngora, on the other hand, rejects it. Even as he erects his cunning backcloth of illusion, in an endeavour to make out of art a substitute for life, he admits to the vanity of his endeavour. His pessimism is absolute.

Gongorism is an exclusively Spanish phenomenon, since only in Spain and her dominions was the rejection of this world in favour of another, which was not directly apprehended, an habitual poetic attitude. The French and German poets, whom we have noticed in our second chapter, were obsessed by the idea of mortality, but revolted against it. Góngora and his followers, on the other hand, perfectly observed the cult of death. Indeed many of their best poems were necrologies. Having extended the 'radiation' of their poetry to the widest area of allusion, they inevitably returned to a single point, man's certain end. Their refusal 'to look', in Wölfflin's words, 'to one side only' is explained by their haunting consciousness of what they would see if once they fixed their eyes. Gongorism is consequently the poetry of the shifting gaze.

[1] Pale death will finally, in the course of time, stroke your breasts with his cold hand.

5

Gardens and landscapes

Plagued by agonized intimations that the world was illusion and life no more than a brightly coloured dream, the Baroque poet was driven to seek refuge either in metaphysical speculation or in imaginary Edens. Moreover, since the original Eden was a garden, and it was to the country that the Renaissance man had longed to withdraw, forsaking court and camp after the Roman fashion, the country and the formal garden became for the seventeenth century a symbol of inward as of outward quiet. Du Bellay voiced a sentiment common to all the members of the Pléiade when he spoke, in his most famous sonnet, of his longing to return, like Ulysses from his long voyage, to the walled garden of his ancestral home in the little town of Liré on the Loire:

> Quand revoirai-je, hélas, de mon petit village
> Fumer la cheminée: et en quel saison
> Revoirai-je le clos de ma pauvre maison,
> Qui m'est une province et beaucoup d'avantage?[1]

Marvell develops the thought much further. His is not a longing, but a state of mental and physical peace, which he is experiencing even as he writes his poems. It is not to his own 'clos', it is true, that he has escaped, if only temporarily, in 'The Garden', from the metaphysical disputes and civil war that afflicted his country. Even as he sits in the garden of

[1] When, alas, shall I see again the chimney of my little village smoking; and in what season shall I see again the walled garden of my poor house, which is a province to me and much besides?

Appleton House, the seat of his patron, the Parliamentary general Lord Fairfax, he is amazed by his private peace and happiness:

> What wond'rous Life is this I lead!
> Ripe Apples drop about my head;
> The Luscious Clusters of the Vine
> Upon my Mouth do crush their Wine;
> The Nectaren, and curious Peach,
> Into my hands themselves do reach;
> Stumbling on Melons, as I pass,
> Insnar'd with Flow'rs, I fall on Grass.
> Meanwhile the Mind, from pleasure less,
> Withdraws into its happiness:
> The Mind, that Ocean where each kind
> Does streight its own resemblance find;
> Yet it creates, transcending these,
> Far other Worlds, and other Seas;
> Annihilating all that's made
> To a green Thought in a green Shade.

This garden is, as I have said, a refuge for the mind afflicted by metaphysical anxieties, and for the man of action involved in the Civil War. Marvell, a man of fundamental tolerance, had taken sides against King Charles, yet in one of his finest poems he commemorated the courage of that monarch upon the block. He was, in fact, unlike du Bellay, and like Quevedo, whose statesmanlike advice to the new favourite we have noted in commenting on his 'Epístola satírica', a man of strong political interests. The latter part of his life indeed was given not to poetry but to a post in Cromwell's Secretaryship of Foreign Tongues (the ancestor of the Foreign Office), and, after the Restoration, to his membership of Parliament for Hull. The political applications of Marvell's garden image emerge most clearly from a passage in his long poem 'Upon Appleton House'. Using a sustained conceit, he first reviews the scene in its martial aspect:

> See how the Flow'rs as at Parade,
> Under their Colours stand displaid:
> Each Regiment in order grows,
> That of the Tulip Pinke and Rose,

and then pleads for the restoration of that primal serenity in which

> The Gardiner had the Souldiers place,
> And his more gentle Forts did trace.
> The Nursery of all things green
> Was then the only Magazeen.
> The Winter Quarters were the stoves,
> Where he the tender Plants removes.

In contrast, that most remarkable of Spanish gardens, described by Marvell's contemporary, Pedro Soto de Rojas, in his 'Paraíso cerrado para muchos, jardines abiertos para pocos' ('Paradise closed to many, gardens open to few'), is all war; his fountains take the form of battleships and castles, and discharge their jets like artillery at all beholders, dealing them, however, only wounds of pleasure and amazement:

> La pertinaz galante artillería,
> Con el humo de balas, que son perlas,
> Moja las luces del amante día,
> Y si la noche mereció cogerlas,
> Morena, pero hermosa,
> Con pabellón de aljófares reposa,
> Y entre faroles de cristal luciente,
> Todo plata respira combatiente,
> Artificiosas mina, y contra mina,
> Preñadas de materia cristalina,
> Quiebran si llegan al parir la fuente,
> De Naya hermosa sucesión corriente.[1]

[1] The persistent and gallant artillery damps the lights of the loving day with its vapour of bullets which are pearls, and if night deserved to catch them, dark but beautiful, he rests in a tent of pearly dewdrops, and between lanterns of gleaming crystal all silver breathes of battle. Cunning mine and countermine, pregnant with crystalline matter, break when they come to bring forth the fountain, the continuously flowing offspring of the fair Naiad.

Rousset has described the fountain as a Baroque symbol for the flux of life[1] which, once the mechanism has been started by the finger of Descartes' rational deity, seemed to the seventeenth century likely to continue for ever. Rojas' poem continues in this manner, sometimes, as in the opening lines of our quotation, with some disregard for syntax, punctuation, and exactness of statement, one image calling up another until Nature is reduced to a perpetual fountain of artifices. The poet's descriptive sense, however, is even more precise than Góngora's in his more visionary 'Soledades', which were undoubtedly the model for the 'Paraíso cerrado'. Rojas' garden on the Albaicín in Granada no longer exists, yet it could be reconstructed, grotto by grotto, statue by statue, and fountain by fountain, with its every tree, shrub, flower, and bearded moss from the sharp pictorial detail of the poem.[2]

Marvell too uses the simile of artillery in his 'Appleton House', in order to describe the levelling of the spectator's eyes from Lord Fairfax's garden on to the neighbouring residence of the Archbishop of York:

> The sight does on these Bastions ply,
> Th' invisible artillery;
> And at proud Cawood Castle seems
> To point the Battery of its Beams.

In his endeavour to remove the whole scene, however, from the stage of reality into that of contemplation or art, he goes on to anticipate Swift in juggling with the relativity of size. His mowers, thus reduced to harmlessness, are seen as grasshoppers entering the tall meadows of grass in which, by contrast, the peaceable and mocking grasshoppers, perched on the heads of the grass-blades, seem to be giants:

> And now to the Abbyss I pass
> Of the unfathomable Grass,
> Where Men like Grashoppers appear,
> But Grashoppers are Giants there;

[1] Op. cit., part ii, passim.
[2] See Emilio Orozco, '*Introducción a un poema barocco granadino*', pp. 43–4 and passim.

> They, in their squeaking laugh, contemn
> Us as we walk more low then them,
> And, from the Precipices tall
> Of the green spires, to us do call.

Thus Marvell, like Rojas, reduces Nature to artificiality. His, however, is a more individual vision, founded rather on an Alice-in-Wonderland transformation of what he sees and hears than on a visual elaboration like that of the poet of the 'Paraíso cerrado'. Nevertheless Marvell also is liable at times to write in a Gongoristic convention that seems to owe nothing to anything actually seen. The opening of 'On a Drop of Dew', which like 'The Garden' he first wrote in Latin, seems to be a free variation on a theme several times treated by Góngora in his early sonnets:

> See, how the Orient Dew,
> Shed from the Bosom of the Morn
>   Into the blowing Roses,
> Yet careless of its Mansion new,
> For the clear Region where 'twas born,
>   Round in its self incloses:
>   And, in its little Globes Extent,
> Frames as it can, its native element.

One is reminded not of any rose that ever grew in a garden but of a flower-piece by a skilful Dutch painter, in which a bead of dew on one petal is made to reflect objects in the room which lie outside the painter's line of sight.

Unlike Góngora, with whose poetry he must undoubtedly have become familiar during his youthful sojourn in Madrid, Marvell does not go on to consider the remorseless passage of time and the inevitable wilting of the flower, but develops a scientific conceit: his dewdrop imitates the shape of the universal sphere from which it fell, and of which it is the microcosm, and therefore forgets that it may in the end fall off the petal.

Rojas' method is by contrast self-elaborating. The first simile leads to the second. The fountain first appears as a vapour of pearly bullets, then by a further twist of artificiality as a tent of pearls, and next by an extremely complicated conceit which appeals straight to the eyes, without recourse to the reason, as a series of mines and countermines from which the jet springs like a new-born child. Rojas does not appeal to the visual imagination alone. By the boldest use of synaesthesia, he causes bird-songs to pierce the ears like arrows and scent of jasmine:

> Verdes las calles, cándidos arqueros,
> Bravos soldados de jazmín florido,
> Cupidillos de amor llenos de antojos,
> Dulces rayos apuntan a los ojos
> Del olfato, y disparan al sentido.[1]

While Góngora's whole intention in the 'Soledades' was aesthetic, to build a palace of art that would shut out life, Rojas, like Marvell, is drawn by the contemplation of this elaborate garden of the senses to thoughts of the Supreme Gardener, who is for ever creating them:

> Cuya temida mano vencedora
> Retirada se encierra
> Dentro de las entrañas de la tierra,
> Adonde organizando las raíces,
> Con mixtos elementos,
> Con sustancias, humores, calidades,
> Muestra las repetidas variedades
> En los verdes fructíferos sustentos,
> En formas de las flores, y matices,
> Que sin pincel colora,
> Negando al más cuidoso lo imitable.[2]

[1] The walks are green. White archers, brave soldiers of flowering jasmine, little Cupids, full of caprices, point sweet rays at the eyes of the faculty of smell, and shoot at the senses.

[2] Whose dreaded, conquering hand, withdrawn, is buried in the bowels of the earth where, arranging the roots, with blended elements, mixtures of substances, humours, and qualities, he shows the constant varieties in the green crops of fruit, in the forms of the flowers and their hues, which he colours without a brush, defying imitation even by the most careful.

The Divine Gardener was, in fact, more cunning than any human artificer, and Rojas prostrated himself before Him in his last lines, fearing that his praise was overbold,

> Pues cuando vuela más, menos te alcanza.[1]

Marvell was more confident in the Divine Hand which, having once made Eden, still hovered over the garden of Appleton House. He, too, praises the Lord for His skill as an artificer:

> How well the skilful Gardner drew
> Of flow'rs and herbes this Dial new;
> Where from above the milder Sun
> Does through a fragrant Zodiack run;
> And, as it works, th' industrious Bee
> Computes its time as well as we.
> How could such sweet and wholsome Hours
> Be reckon'd but with herbs and flow'rs!

The French writers of poems on solitude, however, the *libertin* poets, Marc-Antoine de Saint-Amant and Théophile de Viau, found no such divine assurance in the contemplation of country and garden scenes.

The word solitude (Spanish, 'soledad'; Portuguese, 'saudade') has for the Iberian peninsula the secondary meaning of sadness or longing for lost friends. This association is absent from Góngora's 'Soledades' which, being rooted in the world of art, show very little feeling. Nothing is lost by the shipwrecked mariner that he could not well do without. Having left the world of courts and battles, and found an island Arcadia, how could he wish to return to the turmoil? Marvell's garden, on the other hand, was only a halting-place from which he would eventually depart with redoubled strength for future action. The Bermudas of his voyages, in which God

---

[1] Since when it flies highest, it comes least close to you.

> hangs in shades the Orange bright,
> Like golden Lamps in a green Night:
> And does in the Pomgranates close,
> Jewels more rich than *Ormus* knows,

lie halfway between the native land which they had forsaken
and the American colonies in which they were to refound their
communities after the Restoration. The calm of Eden was, in
Marvell's view, capable of recapture upon earth, amidst
human society. For, being a balanced and active man, he was
at heart an optimist. The 'Solitudes' of the *libertins,* on the
other hand, were true to the secondary and Iberian meaning
of that word. Theirs is a poetry of night, of overhung gardens,
desolate ruins, and stagnant ponds. Saint-Amant, indeed, in
his 'Solitude' seems to foreshadow the eighteenth century's
love of architectural decay:

> Que j'aime à voir la décadence
> De ces vieux châteaux ruinés,
> Contre qui les ans mutinés
> Ont déployé leur insolence!
> Les sorciers y font leur sabat;
> Les démons follets s'y retirent,
> Qui d'un malicieux ébat
> Trompent nos sens et nous martirent;
> Là se nichent en mille troux
> Les couleuvres et les hiboux.
>   L'orfraie, avec ses cris funèbres,
> Mortels augures des destins,
> Fait rire et dancer les lutins
> Dans ces lieux remplis de ténèbres.
> Sous un chevron de bois maudit
> Y branle le squelette horrible
> D'un pauvre amant qui se pendit
> Pour une bergère insensible,
> Qui d'un seul regard de pitié
> Ne daigna voir son amitié.[1]

[1] How I love to see the decay of those old, ruined castles against which
the rebellious years have martialled their insolence! Wizards hold their

These desolate woodlands show little evidence of the poet's natural observation. They are more closely related to the dream-like charnel-house landscapes of our second chapter than to the clear goatherds' island of the 'Soledades', or the gardens of Marvell and Rojas. De Viau, in the third ode of his 'Maison de Sylvie', describes a landscape that is in some ways similar to, but that calls up no associations with, a witches' sabbath. It reveals rather that yearning to escape into the far-away past which pervades such paintings of his contemporary Claude le Lorrain as 'The Marriage of Isaac and Rebecca' in the National Gallery. Here the dancing of the wedding party in the foreground is secondary to the great expanse of water that stretches back, interrupted only by the gentle ripple with which it falls from one level to another into the far distance. Such, Claude seems to say, was the softness of the Bible landscape, which symbolized for him the married happiness of the patriarch. His streams or fountains are gentler even than those which feed Saint-Amant's pool:

> Un étang dort là tout auprès,
> Où ces fontaines violentes
> Courent, et font du bruit exprès
> Pour éveiller ses vagues lentes.
> Lui d'un maintien majestueux
> Reçoit l'abord impetueux
> De ces Naïades vagabondes,
> Qui dedans ce large vaisseau
> Confondent leur petit ruisseau
> Et ne discernent plus ses ondes.
>
> Là Mélicerte, en un gazon
> Frais de l'étang qui l'environne,
> Fait aux Cygnes une maison
> Qui lui sert aussi de couronne.

sabbaths and bogeys return there, who trick our senses and tease us with their malicious pranks. There vipers and owls nest in a thousand holes.

The sea-eagle, with its funereal cries by which the fates prophesy death, makes the elves laugh and dance in these shadow-filled places. Beneath a beam of accursed wood swings the horrible skeleton of a poor lover who hanged himself for a callous shepherdess, who did not deign to grant his friendship a single piteous glance.

> Si la vague qui bat ses bords
> Jamais avec des trésors
> N'arrive à son petit Empire,
> Au moins les vents et les rochers
> N'y font point crier les nochers
> Dont ils ont brisé les navires.[1]

This is a landscape of absolute peace. It represents the refuge into which the unfortunate de Viau hoped one day to retire from the dangers and embarrassments of his disorderly life. He has, at moments, a sharper eye for detail than his Spanish or Italian contemporaries. Perhaps the temperate French landscape offers more to the poet's eye. Nevertheless de Viau is following the technique of Góngora, whose early sonnets were no doubt known to him, when he describes the round house that the god builds for the swans as 'serving him also as a crown'. Visually it may be imagined as crowning the bank and overhanging the water. But his conceit is less carefully worked out than that of Marvell in which he compares the bundled stooks of a hayfield to rocks lying in the calm sea of the stubble:

> When after this 'tis piled in Cocks,
> Like a calm Sea it shows the Rocks:
> We wondring in the River near
> How boats among them safely steer.
> Or, like the Desert Memphis Sand,
> Short Pyramids of Hay do stand.

Having first compared his stooks to rocks, Marvell goes on to describe them as small pyramids in the desert, and then as hill-top tumuli, which the archaeologists of his day identified with the sites of Roman camps. Here, in Marvell's description

[1] A pool sleeps close by into which strong fountains flow, making a deliberate noise to wake their slow waves. With majestic calm it receives the headlong attacks of these vagabond nymphs who loose their little streams in this great basin and no longer notice their ripples. The water-god, on a cool lawn, which surrounds the pond, is building a house for the swans, which will also serve him as a crown. If the wave that beats its banks does not come with treasures to his little Empire, at least the winds and the rocks do not draw cries from mariners whose ships they have shattered there.

of the familiar in terms of the unfamiliar, we have not an echo from Góngora but a native English variant of that Gongorist style by virtue of which sheep were transformed into wandering lilies ('errantes lilios').

Marvell is capable also, as Donne was before him, of working out what seems to be an entirely cold conceit. The 'Appleton House' poem ends with one, which is based on a most curious piece of observation. It is as if the poet were unwilling to conclude with the praise of his patron, or rather of his patron's daughter, to whom the last verses have been devoted. Suddenly he feels impelled to point out the artificiality of the whole vision; which he does by stating in a highly figurative manner that evening is falling and it is time for him to break off his poem:

> But now the Salmon-Fishers moist
> Their Leathern Boats begin to hoist;
> And, like Antipodes in Shoes,
> Have shod their Heads in their Canoes.
> How tortoise like, but not so slow,
> These rational Amphibii go!
> Let's in: for the dark Hemisphere
> Does now like one of them appear.

The picture of the fishermen lifting their coracles and placing them on their heads is hardly the most likely to suggest the fall of evening. In fact the mere cessation of their fishing has already done so, and the elaboration tends rather to deflect the reader's attention than to reinforce the message. Yet if one thinks of Marvell's ending as a deliberate and Baroque attempt to stress the fictitious and pictorial nature of reality we see that its wanton artificiality is absolutely right. Throughout the poem, as in Rojas' 'Paraíso cerrado', everything has been described in terms of something else; flower-beds in terms of regiments drawn up in battle, and the grazing cattle as fleas on a huge looking-glass landscape. Even the stars appear as soldiers:

> the vigilant Patroul
> Of stars walks round about the Pole.

It is right, therefore, that Marvell should thus end his poem with the most far-fetched conceit of all.

Seventeenth-century painters had already developed a sense of landscape. The figures in the foreground of Rubens' great 'Château de Steen' in the National Gallery have only a minor significance. The castle itself is no more than a harshly lit side-drop that is not intended to deflect the spectator's eye for long from the true drama. For what interested the painter was the recession of field and woodland, of rutted roads, pollarded trees, and rough banks that lead one back to a flat horizon, lying under thin clouds. A tree-lined avenue, like Hobbema's in his 'Grove at Middelharnis', also in the National Gallery, or a vast area of field and fen, stretching beneath a cloudy sky to that dim line where sky, sea, and land meet and merge in a blue haze, as in another Hobbema canvas, affords a drama without human interest that is Baroque in its concentration on depth and movement. Ruysdael, as a painter of storm at sea, concerns himself primarily with the violence of wind, sky, and water, and entirely omits to dramatize the sailor whose life is in peril in his storm-tossed craft.

Poets, however, failed to approach Nature so directly until the end of the eighteenth century. Saint-Amant, for instance, who in other poems than his 'Solitude' showed a keen sense of landscape, painted the country as mere background scenery to human activities. His set of four sonnets on the seasons in different climates not only put man in the foreground but tend, after the manner of Poussin, to mythologize him. Even when he writes of autumn in the Canaries, which lie outside the Classical world, he refers to their grapes and fruit as 'the glory of Bacchus and Pomona'. His fruit do not hang on the trees like Marvell's oranges, but 'crown the bibulous god':

> Les figues, les muscats, les pêches, les melons
> Y couronnent ce dieu qui se délecte à boire;
> Et les nobles palmiers, sacrés à la victoire,
> S'y courbent sous des fruits qu'au miel nous égalons.[1]

[1] Figs, muscats, peaches, melons, there crown the bibulous god, and the noble palm-trees, sacred to victory, bow beneath that fruit which we compare to honey.

It is odd that when thinking of the palm as a provider of honey-sweet dates Saint-Amant must still make perfunctory mention of its associations with victory. Classical associations die hard. Although a 'modern poet' and a *libertin*, Saint-Amant seems to have looked at these African islands through the spectacles of Classical culture. The best of this set, 'L'Hiver des Alpes', though bolder in its imagery, suggests not so much a mountain landscape in winter as the background of a carefully constructed Classical crib, in which the Holy Birth has taken place in a northern winter.

> Ces atomes de feu qui sur la neige brillent,
> Ces étincelles d'or, d'azur et de cristal
> Dont l'hiver, au soleil, d'un lustre oriental
> Pare ces cheveux blancs que les vents éparpillent;
> Ce beau coton du ciel de quoi les monts s'habillent
> Ce pavé transparent fait du second metal
> Et cet air net et sain, propre à l'esprit vital,
> Sont si doux à mes yeux que d'aise ils en pétillent.
> Cette saison me plaît, j'en aime la froideur;
> Sa robe d'innocence et de pure candeur
> Couvre en quelque façon les crimes de la terre.
> Aussi l'Olympien la voit d'un front humain;
> Sa colère l'épargne, et jamais le tonnerre
> Pour désoler ses jours ne partit de sa main.[1]

The sparks on the snow, the personified winter, the clear silver ice on road or river; all have a pleasant and miniature charm. There is less artificiality here than in a country scene by Góngora or Marvell, and there is less curious originality

[1] These atoms of fire that shine on the snow, these sparks of gold, blue and crystal with which winter, in the sun, with an eastern lustre, decorates his white hair that is blown apart by the winds; this lovely cotton from the sky with which the mountains are clothed. This transparent pavement made of the second metal [silver] and this clean, healthy air, which suits the vital spirits, are so soft to my eyes that they sparkle with pleasure. This season pleases me, I love its coldness; its robe of innocence and pure candour to some extent covers the crimes of the earth. So the Olympian takes a kindly view of earth. His anger spares it, and the thunder has never left his hands to spoil its days.

than in the seascape by Bocángel, in which the convict blows his trumpet to proclaim that the day's work has ended. But still there is no direct approach to Nature, whom the Baroque poets seem to have loved best when she acted most violently. Earthquake and volcanic eruption are favourite themes of the Marinists, who found in these catastrophic events an objective counterpart to their own inner unrest, which they never expressed directly. Ciro di Pers, however, in the second of his two sonnets on an earthquake, not only dramatizes the disaster but makes it point a moral:

> la terra vacilla, a cui pesanti
> son troppo omai le gravi colpe umane;
> e noi, dormendo, pur con l'ombre vane
> stiamo a scherzar de' lievi sogni erranti.[1]

Pers, who had a strong sense of the vanity of life and the deceptiveness of all human greatness, drew a similar moral from a spring day of unaccustomed sultriness:

> Fresc' aura per lo ciel volo non stende:
> ché incenerite ha l'ale a tanto ardore.
> Langue la messe, e di piovoso umore
> in van ristoro a la sua sete attende.
> Fervido è 'l Tauro, e di gran fiamma ardente
> ne promette il Leon. Deh, quale intanto
> soccorso avrà la sbigottita gente?
> Di far pietoso il ciel non si dia vanto:
> ché s'a placarlo è'l pianto sol possente,
> omai ne gli occhi inaridito è'l pianto.[2]

[1] The earth shakes, since the weight of grievous human crimes is too much for it, and we, asleep, are still playing with the vain shadows of light, wandering dreams.

[2] Fresh air does not extend its flight through the sky, for its wings have been burnt by so much heat. The crop is limp, and waits in vain for the rain to refresh its thirst. Taurus [April] is hot, and Leo [August] promises great burning fires. Alas, what help meanwhile will there be for the anxious people? Let no one boast of being able to make the heavens merciful, for though only tears are strong enough to placate it, the tears are already exhausted in our eyes.

Pers' attitude is, at bottom, pagan. Man who lives under the burning signs was at the beginning moulded by Prometheus from clay moistened with tears:

> Mentre l'uomo formò, Prometeo forse
> il duro fango distemprò col pianto,
> e co' sospir lo spirito gli porse.[1]

Although images can be found in the poetry of Ciro di Pers, as in that of many other Baroque poets, that seem to look forward to Romanticism, in his feeling for Nature this most direct and original of Marino's followers is closer to Platonism than to the empathy of Wordsworth and Leopardi. For it is not Nature herself that engages his interest but the impersonal forces which appear to work through her. Bocángel is even further from making a fresh transcript from reality in his sonnet on an eruption of Vesuvius, about which he had read in a book. This late Gongorist, who was essentially a poet of the study or library, immediately placed the disaster in its Olympian context. Then, with a pessimism not unlike that of Pers, he acquitted both Neptune and Jupiter of all responsibility for the event, which he attributed more justly to the violence already present in the hearts of its victims:

> Ardió el Vesuvio aquí; no la inclemencia
> de Júpiter honró su infiel desmayo,
> ni a rayos de agua le anegó el Tridente.
> El que tiene por alma la violencia
> no ha menester para morir el rayo,
> pues nace fulminando un accidente.[2]

Nature, though kind in Marvell's eyes and callous in Bocángel's, is for both alike governed by artifice. For both, as for Descartes, her principles are those of a machine. For it was

---

[1] When he shaped man Prometheus probably softened the hard clay with tears, and breathed in his spirit with sighs.

[2] Here Vesuvius flames; Jupiter's severity did not greet his [man's] lapse from faith, nor did the Trident [Neptune] drown him in floods. He who has violence in place of a soul has no need of a thunderbolt to die, for, like lightning, a chance event arises.

the Baroque age that saw the birth of objective science, and the emergence of pure mathematics and dynamics. It is important, however, when contrasting the Metaphysicals with the Marinists and Gongorists, to remember that whereas this new attitude to reality had been gaining adherents in England since the time of Francis Bacon, it was rigorously excluded from Spain and Italy, where the theological basis of all knowledge was insisted on.

Marvell, therefore, looking into the depths of the grass, drew his own subjectively scientific conclusions as to the relative height of men and grasshoppers. But Marino, in a passage of comparable beauty in 'L'Adone' (canto VII, 32–3), starts from a poetic cliché, which goes back at least as far as Claudian, when he speaks of the nightingale as 'the siren of the woods':

> Ma sovr' ogni augellin vago e gentile
> che più spieghi leggiadro il canto e 'l volo,
> versa il suo spirto tremulo e sottile
> la sirena de'boschi, il rosignuolo;
> e tempra in guisa il peregrino stile
> che par maestro de l'alato stuolo.
> In mille fogge il suo cantar distingue,
> e trasforma una lingua in mille lingue.
>
> Udir musico mostro, oh meraviglia,
> che s'ode sì ma si discerne apena,
> come or tronca la voce, or la ripiglia,
> or la ferma, or la torce, or scema, or piena,
> or la mormora grave, or l'assottiglia,
> or fa di dolci groppi ampia catena,
> e sempre, o se la sparge o se l'accoglie,
> con egual melodia la lega e scioglie.[1]

[1] But above all the sweet and lovely birds that display a more delicate song and flight, the siren of the woods, the nightingale, pours forth its tremulous and subtle soul, and so tunes its rare note as to seem the master of the winged tribe. It divides its song into a thousand shapes, and transforms one tongue into a thousand. How marvellous to hear this musical prodigy, which is heard but scarcely seen! Now it cuts short its song and then resumes it! Now it stops, now it trills! Now it is soft, now loud! Now it fades, now utters a long chain of sweet phrases, and always, whether scattering them or holding them back, it binds and looses them with equal melody.

This stock Latin theme of the singing contest between the birds had lately been treated in hexameters by the Jesuit poet Famiano Strada. It was a favourite subject for the Latin poets of the time. Marino, however, in his Italian version, although incorporating it in his vast poem whose subject was ostensibly Classical, sought to acclimatize it to his age and country. He called many of the birds by their local Italian names, and placed his singing contest among the boughs of an ancient oak-forest. Nevertheless it is clear that he was thinking of the music of human singers. Not only does he use the terms of the new music (*contrapunteggian*, *ricercati*, and, in one of the stanzas quoted, *groppi*) but his whole passage suggests the rise and fall, and the interlocked phrasing, of a madrigal by Marino's great contemporary, Claudio Monteverdi. The virtues of 'L'Adone' lie largely in its word-music.

The most Italianate of the English Metaphysicals, Richard Crashaw, himself a translator of Marino, working a similar theme, took some fifteen lines of Strada's poem as the principal basis for the hundred or more of his 'Musick's Duel', which he devoted to the contest between 'the siren of the woods' and a human lute-master. His nightingale, however, even more certainly than Marino's, is really a female soprano in feathery disguise. One is reminded of the dying Clorinda in Monteverdi's 'Combattimento':

> her supple Brest thrills out
> Sharpe Aires, and staggers in a warbling doubt
> Of dallying sweetnesse, hovers ore her skill,
> And folds in wav'd notes with a trembling bill,
> The plyant Series of her slippery song.
> Then starts she suddenly into a Throng
> Of short thicke sobs, whose thundering volleyes float,
> And roule themselves over her lubricke throat
> In panting murmurs, still'd out of her Breast
> That ever-bubling spring; the sugred Nest
> Of her delicious soule, that there does lye
> Bathing in streames of liquid Melodie;

Musicks best seed-plot, whence in ripend Aires
A golden-headed Harvest fairely reares
His Honey-dropping tops, plow'd by her breath
Which there reciprocally laboureth
In that sweet soyle.

In the first half of this quotation Crashaw appears to be following the actual trill of the nightingale's song. But soon he begins to perform 'a metaphorical exercise'. The bird's breast is transformed into a distilling retort, a spring, a nest (which turns into a bath), a plot of ground that is ploughed, seeded, and harvested; and finally it becomes an angel-choir in a cathedral, which complains that men should lie in bed while it performs its matins. The poem is in fact personal. Its subject is the effect of song upon the poet himself. Strada's fable is forgotten, and we are invited 'to hear the music, and also to see it, to sniff its sweet odour, to swill its cream and its sugar, to float upon its streams of melody'.[1]

Crashaw and Marino view Nature through the lenses of literary convention, which cast a green shade that is not exactly the natural green. First-hand landscape drawing like that of Hobbema, Koninck, Rubens, and Ruysdael is as rare in the Baroque poets as true self-portraiture after the manner of Rembrandt. Though what they see lies close to reality, yet it has always been altered to suit a traditional picture. It is surprising, therefore, to find a miniature observation, like that of Claudio Acchilini in his sonnet on the wood in spring, which is made to say to the reclining shepherd:

A te m'inchino, a te verdeggio;
e l'ombre mie la giovinetta foglia
tesse col sole e ti ricama il seggio.[2]

Too often, however, the poet refuses to use his eyes, but repeats such faulty observations, based perhaps on Pliny's *Natural History*, as that in Marino's sonnet 'Dipartita', by

[1] See Austin Warren, *Crashaw*, pp. 109–10.
[2] Towards you I bow, for you I grow green, and the young foliage weaves its shadows with the sun, and embroiders your seat.

which the roots of plants that have been parted stretch out to one another underground:

> E due piante talor divise stanno;
> ma sotterra però con le radici
> se non co' rami, a ritrovarsi vanno.[1]

Like Crashaw's sobbing nightingale, the severed plant is seen to emulate the conduct of men.

The walled garden of his childhood's home, for which du Bellay longed during his exile in the harsh, grasping, artificial capital of the religious world, was the refuge desired by every poet of the Baroque age. All, by their choice of themes, showed that they preferred the country to the town, the farmer's life to the courtier's. Yet none was capable of making a true reading from Nature; all saw her through the medium of books. It was left to the poet of that age whose lyrical manner was least affected by Baroque techniques, but was rather a prolongation of the popular Elizabethan tradition, to give a straightforward account of those country pleasures from which the seventeenth-century courtier-poet found himself debarred:

> To hear the Lark begin his flight,
> And singing startle the dull night,
> From his watch-towre in the skies,
> Till the dappled dawn doth rise;
> Then to com in spight of sorrow,
> And at my window bid good morrow,
> Through the Sweet-Briar, or the Vine,
> Or the twisted Eglantine.
> While the cock with lively din,
> Scatters the rear of darkness thin,
> And to the stack, or the Barn dore,
> Stoutly struts his Dames before,
> Oft list'ning how the Hounds and horn
> Chearly rouse the slumbring morn,
> From the side of some Hoar Hill
> Through the high wood echoing shrill.

[1] And sometimes two plants stand divided; nevertheless, if not with their boughs yet underground they strive to rejoin one another with their roots.

John Milton had the advantage that at least three great English poets before him—Chaucer, Spenser, and Shakespeare —could show him how to record the simple face of Nature. True, many Renaissance poets in other countries—Ronsard, Garcilaso, and even Tasso—had made contact with the fields and woods and waters of their native lands, but with the Counter-Reformation a greater separation was established between pagan nature and potentially pagan man. The Baroque poets, therefore, substituted a series of elaborate anamorphoses which appeared truthful only when viewed through the green spectacles of their own illusions concerning the real world. In setting art above reality they lost sight of the world of forest and stream, of moor and mountain, of seedtime and harvest. Du Bellay would never again see his chimney smoking, nor Quevedo forsake the hurly-burly of political intrigue and resume the simple and austere life of his ancestors. Fresh contact with Nature was a hundred and fifty years away.

6

Donne's elephant and Donne's courtier

WHILE it is true that the Baroque poet failed to make as immediate an approach to Nature as the Baroque painter, his curiosity concerning the world of man, beast, and plant developed rather more fully, though in a somewhat piecemeal fashion, for he was still so much influenced by the Platonic method that he was more concerned with principles than with single objects. The sixteenth century had aimed at the co-ordination of its sciences. Mme de Mourgues notes three attempts in France alone to compile 'a versified encyclopedia of human knowledge', of which Ronsard's early 'Hymnes' came nearest to success. But these 'Towers of Babel', she concludes, 'raised high as the stars by the pride of the Renaissance . . . were to share the fate of that Tower. With an ardent desire for order, they collected all the materials available; philosophy, theology, physics, astronomy, mathematics, arts . . . and, piling them up, endeavoured to explain away all the metaphysical contradictions and to rejoice in the harmony of the whole.'[1]

The Baroque poet was less ambitious. Probably he had no belief in this inherent harmony. Nevertheless he persisted in relating one thing to another. Though the range of his interests was wider than that of the Renaissance poet, who seldom undertook any examination for which he could not find a precedent among the Greeks and Romans, he rarely considered anything for its innate qualities. There are few if any Baroque poets of whom the critic can say, as Martin Soria does of the Spanish Baroque painter Francisco Zurbarán,

[1] See *Metaphysical, Baroque and Précieux Poetry*, p. 32.

that 'where he is concerned with objects, he gives them life, treating them with a tenderness, a sense of uniqueness that is wholly refreshing . . .'[1] Zurbarán could turn from contemplating the monk, ecstatic in his prayers, to consider the loaf, the wine-jar, and the cup. 'He only saw the essential,' continues Soria, 'and this he saw with greatness.'[2]

In one respect, however, Zurbarán was a less Baroque figure than the French poet Guillaume du Bartas, who by date belongs more properly in the late Renaissance, since he died in 1590, eight years before Zurbarán was born. For in his vast poem on the seven days of Creation du Bartas broke the Renaissance vision of unity which Zurbarán preserved both in his religious painting and in his still-life, where his serenity is in complete contrast to the constant state of convulsion and metamorphosis which, as Wölfflin noted, is a usual characteristic of the Baroque. The last of the Pléiade, du Bartas reduced that school's vision of order to a rhetorical succession of picturesque moments, separated by passages of grandiose apostrophe and moralizing. He was, in fact, the Victor Hugo of his century. He was at the same time, however, the last of the scientific poets, in succession to Maurice Scève and Ronsard, who had endeavoured to see the universe as a whole. He is comprehensive, therefore, even if he achieves no unity, having no such dramatic myth as John Milton, whose plan for *Paradise Lost* was, nevertheless, a little influenced by Sylvester's English translation of du Bartas' poem. For whereas the Fall and Redemption of man are essentially dramatic subjects, the creation of the world is merely episodic: in du Bartas' treatment a matter of one thing following another. In his failure to suggest any inner connection between the various beasts whose creation he described, du Bartas, before the Baroque age, contributed heavily to its typical fragmentation of vision.

The fifth day of creation, on which God made the birds and fishes, gave du Bartas a sublime opportunity for the display

[1] *Art and Architecture in Spain and Portugal, 1500–1800* (Pelican History of Art), p. 242.
[2] Op. cit., p. 243.

of his curious and often inaccurate knowledge, for much of which he probably relied on Pliny's *Natural History*. In his language, however, he somewhat cacophonously anticipates the high Baroque with its broken rhythms, its elaborate and sometimes heavy word-play, and its scientific or colloquial vocabulary. Du Bartas is so far from presenting a calm and unified picture of the Universe that such a typical passage as that which he devotes to the legendary remora or sucking-fish, which was believed to be capable of staying the course of any ship to which it might attach itself, ends in some disorder with a pair of rhetorical questions. On the whole, however, du Bartas was both credulous and circumstantial:

> La Rémore fichant son débile museau
> Contre le moite bout du tempêté vaisseau,
> L'arrête tout d'un coup au milieu d'une flotte
> Qui suit le vueil du vent et le vueil du pilote:
> Les rênes de la nef on lâche tant qu'on peut,
> Mais la nef pour cela charmée ne s'émeut,
> Non plus que si la dent de mainte ancre fichée
> Vingt pieds dessous The'tis la tenait accrochée:
> Non plus qu'un chêne encor qui, des vents irrités
> A mille et mille fois les efforts dépités,
> Ferme, n'ayant pas moins pour souffrir cette guerre
> De racine dessous, que de branches sur terre.
> Dis-nous, Arrête-nef, dis-nous, comment peux-tu
> Sans secours t'opposer à la jointe vertu
> Et des vents, et des mers, et des cieux, et des gâches?
> Dis-nous en quel endroit, ô Rémore, tu caches
> L'ancre qui tout d'un coup bride les mouvements
> D'un vaisseau combattu de tous les éléments?
> D'où tu prends cet engin? d'où tu prends cette force
> Qui trompe tout engin, qui toute force force?[1]

[1] The remora, pushing his weak snout against the moist bottom of the storm-tossed ship, suddenly stops it in the middle of a fleet which follows the will of the wind and the pilot's will. They loosen the ship's ropes as much as they can. Nevertheless the ship is charmed, and moves no more than if the arms of many anchors held it fast, caught twenty fathoms below the level of Thetis [the sea], no more than an oak, which has a thousand times defied the

Du Bartas does not give the remora time to answer, but immediately introduces the dolphin, who is annoyed at having been so far omitted from the poet's long catalogue of fishes. After retelling the Ovidian story of Arion on the dolphin's back, du Bartas then passes on to consider God's creation of the birds. Here, in anticipation of the Baroque commonplace treated in our last chapter, he singles out the nightingale and expatiates on those duels of song at the conclusion of which

> souvent le vaincu porte si grand' envie
> A l'honneur du vainqueur, qu'il perd et voix et vie
> Tout en même moment . . .[1]

Though du Bartas' poem contains many such pictures as that of the remora, and many such unanswerable questions, few of them are as graphic as Donne's symbolic elephant, the emblem of justice and gratitude, in 'The Progresse of the Soule':

> Natures great master-peece, an Elephant,
> The onely harmlesse great thing; the giant
> Of beasts; who thought, no more had gone, to make
>   one wise
> But to be just, and thankfull, loth to offend,
> (Yet nature hath given him no knees to bend)
> Himselfe he up-props, on himselfe relies,
> And foe to none, suspects no enemies,
> Still sleeping stood; vex't not his fantasie
> Blacke dreames; like an unbent bow, carelesly
>   His sinewy Proboscis did remisly lie.

---

force of the angry winds, and remains firm, having as many roots below the soil as branches above it, with which to resist the attack.

Tell us, Ship-stopper, tell us how you can oppose unaided the joint power of the seas, the heavens and the oars. Tell us, remora, where you hide the anchor that suddenly restrains all the movements of a ship beaten by all the elements. Where do you get this mechanism? Where do you get this power that outwits all mechanism, that overpowers all power?

[1] The loser is sometimes so envious of the victor's honour, that he loses voice and life at the same moment.

Donne then goes on to tell Pliny's tale of the envious mouse which entered this proboscis and, coming to the brain, 'gnaw'd the life cords there', whereupon murderer and harmless victim perished together. Donne's poem, a free and satirical speculation on the subject of metempsychosis, is the very opposite of a Renaissance Tower of Babel. For the sole conclusion that it reaches is the relative one, that:

> The onely measure is, and judge, Opinion.

Nor is his elephant any more drawn from life than du Bartas' dolphin, or nightingale, or legendary remora, for Donne could not have seen an elephant in its characteristic kneeling position. Yet the portrait—which may owe something to Dürer—contains the vital quality of vision that is almost totally absent from the first and the unfinished second 'Semaines', which are remarkable rather for their power of language than for poetic invention. Donne postulates his elephant, visualizes it, and, in narrating his fable, isolates it for a moment from the world-picture and draws a lesson from it.

In a similar manner the Marinist poet Girolamo Fontanella, among a number of sonnets devoted to miniature subjects, in which he displays a delicate power of invention, addresses one to the remora in whom he finds a humble virtue comparable to that of Donne's 'onely harmelesse great thing', and thus perhaps answers du Bartas' unanswered question concerning its mechanism:

> Va torreggiante in su le vele a volo
> spedita, a tutto andar, nave corrente;
> di ricche merci e di guerriera gente,
> scorre con aura amica infido suolo;
> quando un picciolo pesce ingordo e solo,
> che furtivo nel mar sorge repente,
> con ancoretta di minuto dente
> le ferma il corso e le ritarda il volo.
> Tanta audacia a costui natura diede,
> tanto poter ne la cerulea corte
> un picciolo animal nutrir si vede.

E

> Così de la virtù vinta è la sorte,
> e suol natura, ove umiltà risiede,
> ne le picciole cose esser più forte.[1]

The remora, like the elephant, is here made to point a moral. The moment for objective vision like that of Zurbarán had not arrived. For that, perhaps, the mystical serenity that is expressed in his holy pictures is necessary. Others of the unmystical Fontanella's sonnets, however, addressed to the glow-worm, the pearl, the coral, and the ermine, and his free odes to the moon, a cicada, the pomegranate, the mouth, the eyes, and the breath, are much more self-sufficient. Though his sonnet on the coral ends with a questioning exclamation, it is less vague and searching than those of du Bartas, and far from metaphysical in its implications:

> Dal tronco il nuotator destro la schianta;
> la prende molle e la ritrova dura,
> e dubbioso non sa s'è pietra o pianta![2]

Fontanella, an obscure Neapolitan, died at the age of thirty-one or two, leaving two books of poems, which have not been reprinted. He was unknown until extracts from them appeared in recent anthologies. Yet of all the Marinists he is the most original in his imagery and the most persistent in his search for new directions. In some sense, indeed, he forestalls that great materialist poet of our own day Pablo Neruda, whose odes addressed to such objects as the onion, the artichoke, etc., attempt to isolate the essential qualities of those

[1] The towering ship scuds onwards in full sail, as fast as it can go; loaded with rich merchandise and martial company, it flies over the treacherous ground [the expanse of sea] with a friendly wind, when a little fish, eager and alone, suddenly and furtively rising from the sea, with its small anchor of tiny teeth, stops and holds back its flight. Such courage has Nature given to this creature. With such power does a little creature find itself provided in the courts of heaven. Thus is fate conquered by virtue, and Nature in which humility dwells is usually stronger in small things.

[2] The skilful diver tears it from the trunk; it is soft when he plucks it, and then he finds it hard, and so he is in doubt, not knowing whether it is a stone or a plant!

objects. Fontanella's technique, however, did not keep pace
with the growth of his invention; too often he used the stock
adjective, and sometimes he drew the stock moral, as in his
second sonnet to the glow-worm, which ends:

> E dirle puoi con amoroso gioco
> che le faville e le tue luci fûro
> i miei sospir che t'infiammâr di foco.[1]

The conceit is a cold one. Fontanella could draw a detailed
picture but could not reason from it. It is along his objective
lines, however, that the new Baroque realism was to develop,
for in his greater detachment from the platonic urge towards
unity of vision Fontanella was a more modern figure than John
Donne, though a poet of much less breadth and mastery.

Giacomo Lubrano, a fellow-Neapolitan and a Jesuit,
carried Fontanella's curious interest in Nature's stranger
creations somewhat further. Not only did he devote a sonnet
to the glow-worm but also to the torpedo, the tarantula, the
swordfish, and the abuse of chilled drinks in hot weather.
Though tempted by his profession to draw a pulpit moral
from each sonnet, Lubrano was original in his choice of
analogies between the world of beasts and that of men. The
glow-worm brings him comfort since when the sky is overcast
its light guides his steps and finds him a path through wild
country. In his natural descriptions he affects the chiaroscuro
that we have found both in the charnel-house poets of the
religious wars and in the Spaniard Jáuregui's description of
Orpheus' descent into hell:

> Vivi baleni e facelline erranti,
> fanno a l'ombre più cieche un chiaro oltraggio,
> e quasi di natura alati incanti,
> cangian le fughe in lampi, il volo in raggio.[2]

[1] And I can tell you in affectionate humour that your sparks and your lights were my sighs, which inflamed you with fire.

[2] Bright lightnings and stray flashes perform a vivid outrage on the deeper darkness, and like winged wonders of nature change their flight into lamps, their flying into rays.

Lubrano's visionary disorder is matched by the violence of his language, which the anthologist G. G. Ferrero has described as delirious. Certainly such bodily disorders as swoon and delirium exercised a fascination over him. Not only did he characterize the torpedo by recounting the lethal results of its sting,

> Di lubrici letarghi oppio squamoso
> e di sincope vive estro guizzante,
> che, vil parto del mar, spira anelante
> gelide epilepsie di verno ondoso,[1]

but he preached a sermon on the even more fatal effects of intemperance when warning a glutton against over-indulgence in wine that has been cooled with snow:

> Ebri epuloni, o voi che in laute cene
> fate brillar voluttüoso il verno,
> ne' dì canicolari entro le vene,
>   tempo verrà che nel profondo Averno
> impetrar non potrete, arsi da pene,
> un'istantanea stilla al foco eterno.[2]

Despite the comfort which Lubrano offers to those of his hearers who heed his lessons, his poetry is essentially pessimistic. The more involved the conceit, the greater the poet's withdrawal from the world of men, and the greater his contempt for it. When Thomas Carew devotes a poem to 'A Mole in Celia's Bosom' we are repelled, despite the delicacy of his language, by the mixture of disgust and arch sensuality with which he speaks of

---

[1] Scaly opium of false stupours, and flashing cause of sharp fainting-attacks, vile spawn of the sea, that breathes gasping, cold epilepsies from the wintry wave.

[2] Drunken gluttons, who make the winter shine voluptuously at your banquets, and in the dog-days introduce it into your veins, there will be a time when, burning with pain in the depths of Avernus, you will not be able to freeze a momentary drop on the eternal fire.

> the aromatic dew,
> Which from the neighbouring vale distils,
> Which parts those two twin-sister hills.

This is not the poetry of love, or even of desire, but of a pessimistic loathing for pleasures enjoyed. The Marinist Giuseppe Artale's sonnet addressed to a flea on a beautiful lady's bottom descends to greater indelicacies, and testifies to a revulsion as extreme and fundamentally as peremptory and unpoetic as Swift's. Certainly Artale does not consider the flea for its own sake or even in relation to his mistress. It is presented only as a symbol for his disgust.

When the Italians discovered the chief curiosities of Nature in the world of the smaller creatures the French and Spaniards looked more directly at human society, which they found even less appealing. The world of the court, as Quevedo describes it, is a human zoo, with each of its inmates behaving like a caricature of itself and occupying a neatly labelled cage. For him human features were as monstrous as those of the animals. In his famous sonnet on the nose, the conceits of which shade over into the common pun, he compared the human proboscis to those of the elephant and the swordfish. He discovered in the world of men deformities which even the more savage of the Marinists had attributed to it only by analogy. Thus the disembodied nose is in itself an animated thing of the kind that Hieronymus Bosch drew in his nightmare altar-pieces:

> érase una nariz sayón y escriba,
> érase un peje espada muy barbado,
>   Era un reloj de sol mal encarado,
> érase una alquitara pensativa,
> érase un elefante boca arriba,
> era Ovidio Nasón más narizado.[1]

Quevedo's nose, unlike Donne's elephant and the Marinists'

[1] It was a constable and scribe of a nose, it was a very hairy swordfish, it was a badly positioned sundial, it was an alembic in deep thought, it was a nosier Ovidius Naso.

glow-worm, points no moral. Its creator takes a purely
negative attitude to society, in which he sees the old pass
themselves off for young, cowards for heroes, and whores for
virgins, while the poor cheat, cuckoldry flourishes, and the
rich are gulled. He does not think of the chameleon, which he
mocks 'moralizando satíricamente su naturaleza' ('drawing a
satirical moral from its nature'), as a real creature, like du
Bartas' or Fontanella's remora. Whatever Pliny may say,
Quevedo knows very well that no creature, and no man either,
can feed on the empty air:

> Dígote pretendiente y cortesano,
> llámete Plinio el nombre que quisiere;
> pues quien del viento alimentarte viere,
> el nombre que te doy tendrá por llano.
>   Fuelle vivo en botarga de gusano,
> glotón de soplos, que tu piel adquiere;
> mamón de la provincia, pues se infiere
> que son tus pechos vara y escribano;
>   si del aire vivieras, almorzaras
> respuestas de ministros y señores;
> consulta y decretos resollaras;
>   fueran tu bodegón aduladores,
> las tontas vendedores de sus caras,
> sastres, indianos, dueñas y habladores.[1]

Such is Quevedo's picture of the common man of his
day. Saint-Amant, whose temperament resembled Quevedo's,
though his devotion to his craft was far less single-minded than
the Spaniard's, took an equally unpleasant view of the world
in which he lived. His Paris, in fact, matches Quevedo's
Madrid: two cities eaten up by the grandeur of the Court and

---

[1] I say that you are a suitor and a courtier, whatever name Pliny may
give you, for anyone who sees you living on air will find the name I bestow
on you quite simple. Living bellows in the breeches of the worm, glutton
for the blasts your skin collects, provincial milksop because it is inferred that
the constable and attorney give you suck, if you lived on air you would
lunch on the answers of ministers and noblemen; you would swallow reports
and decrees; your eating-house would be flatterers, silly women who sell
their faces, tailors, nabobs, landlords and gossips.

crowded with hangers-on, whom the Spaniard satirized as one
of their company and against whom the Frenchman reacted
as 'an outsider'. For he is himself one of the 'guzzlers' of his
sonnet 'Les Goinfres', and he himself had learnt the vice of
prodigality, 'wedged three in a bed without fire or candle':

> Mettre au lieu de bonnet la coiffe d'un chapeau,
> Prendre pour se couvrir la frise d'un manteau
> Dont le dessus servit à nous doubler la panse;
> Puis souffrir cent brocards d'un vieux hôte irrité,
> Qui peut fournir à peine à la moindre dépense,
> C'est ce qu'engendre enfin la prodigalité.[1]

The Baroque poet found the underworld of man as
dangerous and distasteful as the shark-ridden depths of the
sea. Love, ambition, trust, courage, and belief: all were
delusions. It was a world from which satire was about to be
born; and the age that succeeded the Baroque was primarily
an age of satire. There was, however, another possible attitude to the squalor depicted by Quevedo, the running sore on
the breast of the Empire, and this was the compassion evinced
by Velázquez for the clowns and dwarfs and monstrosities
collected by his master Philip IV. Velázquez portrayed each
of them in all his abnormality of limb and feature. Some are
deformed, some half-witted, and some shrewd with a primitive
peasant shrewdness, yet none are despised. It may even be
that one of them served him as a model for Aesop, and another
for Menippus, the two fabulists in the Prado whose simple
dignity seems their sole human quality. All Velázquez' sitters,
clowns and kings alike, are shown not only for what they are
but what they might be. Even the grand poses of Philip IV are
not mocked; he is not shown, as Goya showed his successors,
in all his hollowness and stupidity. Velázquez grants him at
least the aspiration towards kingliness. But it is in the portrayal of his dwarfs and clowns that Velázquez shows the

---

[1] To wear the lining of a hat as a cap, to take the woollen lining of a coat
to cover one and wrap the outside round one's waist, then to put up with a
hundred insults from an angry landlord who can scarcely fill the smallest
order: this is what in the end makes a man prodigal.

height of his patient understanding. All are so well realized that Martin Soria can say of the idiot Calabazas in his Prado portrait that 'by his constrained and crowded pose, he makes you feel his insecurity, his disturbed and repressed condition. . . . That the light of wit has left his face is suggested by the dim lights playing on the countenance and by the eyes set deep in their sockets.'[1]

This compassion, which is sometimes expressed also in the music of the period, most signally in the grief-stricken 'Ora pro nobis' of the 'Sonata supra Sanctae Mariae' in Monteverdi's 'Vespers' of 1610, is entirely missing from the poetry of the Baroque age.

Other characteristics of Velázquez can, however, be found in the poetry of his contemporaries and compatriots. His early 'Borrachos' or 'Topers' translates into earthy terms a theme which his master Titian would have treated in terms of Edenic abstraction from the common world. In this Prado picture a group of boozy Spanish peasants receive in the landscape of the Guadarrama mountains, which lie in the neighbourhood of Madrid, a visit from the young god Bacchus and his naked attendants, whom they welcome on equal terms. Their expressions are kindly, and their behaviour respectful. Yet they do not yield a jot of their natural Spanish dignity. On the contrary, their supernatural visitors appear to have laid aside something of their godlike superiority. Soon, one feels, they will be swapping stories about Jupiter's infidelities.

The spinners of Velázquez' 'Hilanderas', the actual subject of which is the fable of Arachne,[2] are also simple people, as are the water-carrier and the boy at Apsley House, and Martha and Mary in the National Gallery.

Something similar was attempted, though with less complete success, in the poetry of Góngora. Himself far removed, in bookish isolation and neurotic struggle for security, from the common man, Góngora nevertheless attempted to create his own version of this pastoral convention, and display the peasant, in all the oafish oddity of his uncouth language and

[1] Op. cit., p. 263.
[2] Op. cit., p. 269.

coarse habits, as the anti-hero who shows up the sordidness of court and camp. The shipwrecked sailor of the 'Soledades', escaping from an unhappy love-affair, found his Eden on an island inhabited by simple goatherds. In describing his arrival at the goatherd's cottage Góngora stresses that despite its simple architecture it is in fact a temple of the gods, to which he is guided by the barking of the dog and the glow of a woodfire that flickers like a huge butterfly amidst the ashes of their hearth:

> Llegó pues el mancebo, y saludado,
> sin ambición, sin pompa de palabras,
> de los conducidores fué de cabras,
> que a Vulcano tenían coronada.
>   ¡ Oh bienaventurado
>   albergue a cualquier hora,
> templo de Pales, alquería de Flora!
>   No moderno artificio
> borró designios, bosquejó modelos,
> al cóncavo ajustando de los cielos
>   el sublime edificio;
>   retamas sobre roble
>   tu fábrica son pobre,
>   do guarda, en vez de acero,
>   la inocencia al cabrero
>   más que el silbo al ganado.
>   ¡ Oh bienaventurado
>   albergue a cualquier hora![1]

The pastoral convention was taken over by Góngora from the poetry of the Renaissance at a point where it had seemingly been worn threadbare.

[1] Then the youth arrived and was received simply and without grand words by the goatherds who formed a crown for Vulcan [i.e. sat round the fire, of which he was the god]. Oh welcome refuge at any time, temple of Pales [goddess of shepherds] and cottage of Flora! No modern artificer scrawled designs or sketched models in order to fill the vault of heaven with a sublime edifice. Broom laid on oak-trunks was enough for your humble construction, in which innocence in place of arms keeps the goatherd safer than his whistle keeps his flock. Oh welcome refuge at any time! (Translation adapted from the prose version by Dámaso Alonso.)

Tasso's 'Aminta' and Guarini's 'Pastor Fido' had finally exhausted the medium in Italy, and in England Spenser's attempts to make his shepherds talk in country language and obsolete metres had dissolved in absurdity. Nevertheless, the 'other world', in which the simple virtues obtained, cried out to be represented. Milton, with a direct feeling for the country-side, breathed into the artificial framework of his masque 'Comus' a reading of the rural life that he had taken either at first hand from peasants whom he had known or at second hand from Shakespeare, who had been at home in the Warwickshire landscape. But Góngora had to make a fresh start. Born in the harsh and ancient Moorish town of Córdoba, this black-cloaked aristocrat had never known a genial countryside or its simple inhabitants. His poetic language, painfully derived from the artificialities of Herrera, belongs wholly to the realm of literature. Its Latin constructions and hyperbolical figures of speech are many times further from the common idiom than Shakespeare's or Milton's direct English. His peasants had consequently to be conceived anew and could never take on the natural features of those whom Velázquez had observed in the country or at Court. His goat-herds were lay-figures, inherited from Theocritus and Vergil. Yet they embodied his only vision of a better world.

Delighting in the oddities of dialect and accent which he heard around him, Góngora and some of his fellow-poets incorporated them in a kind of mock-antique. The old forms of ballad and carol—*romance* and *villancico*—had fallen into desuetude since Garcilaso's time. Góngora and his generation revived them, often with remarkable success, as a conscious art-form. At the same time Lope de Vega, the best of whose heroes were loyal and shrewd peasants, introduced snatches of folksong, traditional or adapted, into his plays. Góngora, in a more academic way, bringing two shepherds and a negro to perform the Adoration of the Kings, makes each speak in accents distilled if not copied from life:

NEGRO: La Reya mío
                incienso ofrece sagrado.

PASTOR PRIMERO: Humo al fin el humo ha dado.
NEGRO: Sá de Dios al fin presente.
PASTOR PRIMERO: *¿Qué gente, Pascual, qué gente?*
¿Qué polvareda es aquella?
PASTOR SEGUNDO: *La Astrología del Oriente*
cuyo postillón luciente
es una estrella.[1]

This revival of traditional forms by the most self-conscious Baroque technicians unexpectedly brought a short spell of new life to the Spanish lyric. The Italians, who adhered to the old forms, can show nothing to compare with Góngora's *romance* of 'Angélica y Medora', which elaborates a highly sophisticated incident in Ariosto's 'Orlando Furioso'. But like Saint-Amant's winter sonnet, this so-called ballad has all the artificiality of a nativity crib. Built almost entirely of antitheses, it approaches Nature afresh only to retreat to a greater distance. It is Titian rather than Velázquez who provides the visual equivalent of the lovers' marriage bed, for which

Los campos les dan alfombras,
los árboles pabellones,
la apacible fuente sueño,
música los ruiseñores.[2]

Desiring an idyllic society such as he had perhaps glimpsed in childhood, Góngora tried to seek it in Nature but found it only in art.

Quevedo, by contrast, was uneasily at home in the world. He knew how people behaved and talked. He had no need to study the *germanía* or thieves' cant that he introduced into his prose and occasionally into his verse. He had heard it around

[1] NEGRO: MY king offers holy incense. FIRST SHEPHERD: Smoke after all, smoke is what he has given. NEGRO: In the end he'll be witness of a god. FIRST SHEPHERD: What is the crowd, Pascual, what is the crowd? What is that cloud of dust? SECOND SHEPHERD: It's the Eastern Astrology, whose shining outrider is a star.

[2] The fields give them carpets, the trees pavilions, the peaceful fountain gives them sleep, and the nightingales music.

him. But Quevedo was poisoned by hatred of his fellow-men, and of his fellow-poets in particular, among them Góngora. The world of art offered him no refuge. It seemed to him a bear-garden like any other. He could not even admire another man's works, unless, like the Renaissance poet Luis de León, whose forgotten poetry he published, he was safely dead. Taunting Góngora, his greatest contemporary, for his long nose, Quevedo insultingly suggested that he must be of Jewish blood, and punningly demanded that he should cease writing:

> ¿Por qué censuras tú la lengua griega,
> siendo sólo rabí de la judía,
> cosa que tu nariz aun no niega?
>   No escribas versos más, por vida mía;
> que aun aquesto de escribas se te pega,
> pues tienes de sayón la rebeldía.[1]

Though Quevedo had a fine feeling for spoken language, he was far too slapdash in his *romances* and occasional poetry to make finished use of it, and far too furious ever to draw a careful picture of those whom he scorned. His counterpart to Donne's elephant, and to the glow-worms and remora of the Marinists, is a reflection of himself at his angriest, a buzzing mosquito:

> Ministril de las ronchas y picadas,
> mosquito postillón, mosca barbero,
> hecho me tienes el testuz harnero,
> y deshecha la cara a manotadas,
>   Trompetilla que toca a bofetadas,
> que vienes con rejón contra mi cuero,
> Cupido pulga, chinche trompetero,
> que vuelas comezones amoladas,
>   ¿por qué me avisas si picarme quieres?

---

[1] Why do you censure the Greek language, being nothing but a ghetto rabbi, a fact that your nose does not deny? Write no more verses, by my life, because this business of the Scribes still sticks to you, for you are as stubborn as an executioner.

> Que pues que das dolor a los que cantas,
> de casta y condición de potras eres.
>   Tú vuelas, y tú picas, y tú espantas,
> y aprendes del cuidado y las mujeres
> a malquistar el sueño con las mantas.[1]

Quevedo draws no moral but brings the case continually back to himself and his disgust for life. Capable of making the new approach to reality, he did not have the patience to do so; and Spanish poetry did not survive his failure to match his more direct language with an equally direct vision.

English poets, even when their imagery was at its most complex, never entirely forsook spoken rhythms for echoes of Latinity, and never restricted their vision after the Spanish fashion. Donne's flea which, unlike Quevedo's mosquito, existed on more than one plane, having drunk the blood of the two lovers and perished at the hands of one, is allowed to survive as a ghost in order that the poet may use him to point a moral:

> Cruell and sodaine, hast thou since
> Purpled thy naile, in blood of innocence?
> Wherein could this flea guilty bee,
> Except in that drop which it suckt from thee?
> Yet thou triumph'st and saist that thou
> Find'st not thyself nor mee the weaker now;
>   'Tis true, then learne how false, feares bee;
>   Just so much honor, when thou yeeld'st to mee,
>   Will wast, as this flea's death tooke life from thee.

Donne's artificiality may here seem as great as Góngora's. The difference, however, lies in the actuality of Donne's

[1] Minister of weals and stings, outriding mosquito, barber-fly, you have made my forehead a sieve, and destroyed my face with slaps. Little trumpet whose magic is smacks, who comes with a goad against my skin. Cupid-flea, trumpeting louse, that lets fly sharpened stings, why do you warn me if you want to sting me? For since you pain those to whom you sing, you are of the type and nature of a rack. You fly and you sting and you frighten, and you learn from care and women to make sleep dislike blankets. [N.B. Those who confessed on the rack were said to *sing*.]

situation. He is persuading his future wife to give him her virginity. There is, by contrast, hardly more than a single poem of Góngora's which reflects any personal situation at first hand. His finest sonnets and lyrics deplore the passing of beauty and the inexorable march of time, or celebrate the majesty of death. Quevedo, too, who uses most artificiality when writing of love, never reveals any deep experience of it. When he floats on the waves of his mistress's hair we cannot for a moment suppose that, like Donne, he recognizes her as a woman. His Lisis and Amintas have not even the reality of Herrera's platonic mistress.

When Quevedo was airing his spites he was once more defeated by a fundamental lack of emotion. He was angry, but he did not care. Horrified, disgusted, but never implicated or compassionate, he was no more capable of affirming human dignity in the manner of Velázquez than the timid and bookish Góngora. Donne was at times no less cruel, angry, and sardonic. But he had experience of love, both of God and a woman. His 'Satyres', therefore, have a light and shade that is not to be found in Quevedo's ill-tempered, contemptuous, and punning burlesques. He was capable of satire because he knew an alternative to the catch-as-catch-can of bachelor life in the Inns of Court, the London street, and the stews which he had frequented as a young man. Quevedo could only yearn for an imaginary past in which the simple virtues had been honoured. Donne, on the other hand, in his fourth 'Satyre', draws his fashionable, threadbare, and pedantic courtier with some contempt, it is true, but also with a certain pleasure in the manifold absurdities of human nature, which he conveys in the exuberance of his language and the flowing complexities of his metaphors:

> Towards me did runne
> A thing more strange, then on Niles slime, the Sunne
> E'r bred; or all which into Noah's Arke came;
> A thing which would have pos'd Adam to name;
> Stranger than seaven Antiquaries studies,
> Then Africks Monsters, Guianaes rarities,

Stranger than strangers; One, who for a Dane,
In the Danes Massacre had sure been slaine,
If he had liv'd then; And without helpe dies,
When next the Prentises 'gainst Strangers rise.
One, whom the watch at noone lets scarce goe by,
One, to whom, the examining Justice sure would cry,
Sir, by your priesthood tell me what you are.
His clothes were strange, though coarse; and black,
    though bare;
Sleeveless his jerkin was, and it had beene
Velvet, but 'twas now (so much ground was seene)
Become Tufftaffatie; and our children shall
See it plaine Rashe awhile, then nought at all.
This thing hath travail'd, and saith, speakes all tongues
And only knoweth what to all States belongs.
Made of th'Accents, and best phrase of all these,
He speakes no language; If strange meats displease,
Art can deceive, or hunger force my tast,
But Pedants motley tongue, souldiers bumbast,
Mountebankes drugtongue, nor the termes of law
Are strong enough preparatives, to draw
Me to beare this: yet I must be content
With his tongue, in his tongue call'd complement:
In which he can win widdowes, and pay scores,
Make men speake treason, cosen subtlest whores,
Out-flatter favourites, or outlie either
Jovius, or Surius, or both together.
He names mee, and comes to mee; I whisper, God!
How have I sinn'd, that thy wraths furious rod,
This fellow chuseth me?

Donne builds up his portrait at leisure. The words 'strange'
and 'stranger', repeated in their two meanings, throw this
shabby apparition into huge relief. He is the 'pretendiente y
cortesano' of Quevedo's sonnet; he is almost the Spaniard's
disembodied nose. Yet he is at the same time a living figure;
he is neither mythologized in the manner of Góngora nor
depersonalized after the angrier example of Quevedo. Nor

is Donne merely adapting the Latin satire of Persius and
Juvenal to a modern language and modern victims, like his
contemporaries, Joseph Hall, the first English satirist, and
Mathurin Régnier, who occupies a similar place in the history
of French poetry. In his 'Satyres', as in his 'Songs and Sonnets'
and his 'Divine Poems', Donne is a poet of Baroque extravagance and obliquity. But despite his learned breadth of
allusions, he is always colloquial, never literary. Like Quevedo
at his rare best, he is in touch with life. He is at his most
characteristic, indeed, in the bored exclamation with which
this long quotation ended. Its length was dictated by the
leisureliness with which Donne built up his portrait. Dryden
would have required less than half these thirty lines, and
Pope perhaps a quarter. But for all his slow build-up, Donne
scores his individual points with a compression as great as
theirs. The phrase 'montebankes drugtongue', for instance,
translated into prose, would require twice as many words,
denoting as it does, with a certain adenoidal onomatopoeia,
the patter in which sellers of patent medicines advertise their
wares. Again the curious learning with which, after drawing
on Herodotus for his analogy of creatures born from the Nile
mud, and on some chronicler for his reference to the massacre
of the Danes in pre-Conquest London, Donne drops back to
his own century, to recall the London apprentices' mobbing
of foreign craftsmen, is in keeping with the curious perspectives
of the Baroque age. Unlike all the rest that have been quoted
in this chapter, Donne is, in his reading of humanity and the
animal creation, a poet of depth who achieves that 'greater
area of radiation' demanded by Heinrich Wölfflin.

7

The garlands wither

Donne's satirical objectivity and Quevedo's exaspera-
tion were the two features of the Baroque that connected
it most closely with the Classical era that followed. The outstanding poets of this new age, La Fontaine, Dryden, Boileau,
and Pope, were objective and often angry critics of a society
whose emotional horizons had narrowed as its scientific knowledge had increased. From the time of Purcell and Vivaldi
onwards, all deep emotion that found expression in art was
channelled into the stream of music, the most uncommitted
of art-forms. Indeed, this age of music can be viewed as the
consummation of the Baroque. For it is in the combination of
instruments and voices, and of the variety within unity of trio-
sonata, canon, ricercar, and fugue, that the true Baroque
depth, as contrasted with the Classical series of parallel
planes,[1] is to be found.

At the beginning of the Baroque age, on the other hand,
architecture and painting were the predominant forms, and
the prevailing vision was of monumental greatness. Music
followed the rhythm of words or the motions of the feet. Not
till the end of the sixteenth century did the Venetian Giovanni
Gabrieli combine voices and instruments to make their own
sacred patterns; and a few years later Monteverdi and Schütz
gave music its independence both from the church service and
from poetry and the dance.

The Renaissance poet was a close ally of the Renaissance
hero. Sometimes, as in the case of Sir Philip Sidney, the two
men were one. Garcilaso, Spenser, Camões, and many others

[1] See Wölfflin, op. cit., p. 15.

were men of action. Consequently the Renaissance poet believed in the martial virtues, and, subscribing to the myth of
his time, saw in his country and its rulers a likeness to those
of ancient Rome. He believed in their mission to conquer and,
whilst hotly pursuing treasure and profit, to Christianize (or
forcibly convert to their form of Christianity) the inhabitants
of other technically more backward and less fortunate lands.
The Baroque age inherited the mood of measured optimism
in which Camões completed his 'Lusiads'. For it was not in a
state of absolute confidence that he invoked the King of
Portugal's protection for his adventurous vassals, whom he had
followed, in his poem, from exploit to exploit, as in fulfilment
of their country's divinely appointed mission they explored
the eastern world and fought the 'Idolaters and Moors':

> Olhai que ledos vão, por várias vias,
> Quais rompentes leões e bravos touros,
> Dando os corpos a fomes e vigias,
> A ferro, a fogo, a setas e pelouros,
> A quentos regiões, a plagas frias,
> A golpes de Idolatras e de Mouros,
> A perigos incógnitos do mundo,
> A naufrágios, a peixes, ao profundo.[1]

Camões acknowledged, however, that the courage with
which the Portuguese had sailed to India and China under
Vasco da Gama had for some reason diminished:

> E não sei por que influxo de Destino
> Não tem um ledo orgulho e geral gosto,
> Que os ânimos levanta de contino
> A ter para trabalhos ledo o rosto.[2]

[1] Oh, how joyfully they travel on various roads, like charging lions and
brave bulls, giving their bodies to famine and vigils, to sword, fire, arrows
and cannon balls, to hot regions and cold climates, to blows of idolators and
Moors, to the unknown perils of the world, to shipwrecks, fishes and the
deep.

[2] I know not through what influence of Fate there is no longer that
happy pride and general desire that leads men to undergo hardships with
constancy and a cheerful face.

For this decline in his country's valour Camões saw one remedy alone: that the king should set his people a heroic example. Six years later this same king, Don Sebastião o Desejado (the Desired), acting in the spirit that the poet demanded, led an ill-organized army to defeat in Morocco and himself perished in the battle. The first of the new Renaissance powers, mistress of the Indian and China trade routes and of Brazil, was destroyed and her conquests divided between the Spaniards, who annexed the kingdom of Portugal to their crown, and the Dutch, who inherited the Indies.

The defeat of Don Sebastião was celebrated by the first of Spanish Baroque poets, Fernando de Herrera, in a mood of confidence hardly less exhilarated than that with which Camões had begun his Virgilian epic. Herrera believed in the divine destiny of his own people to succeed where the Portuguese had failed. In his 'State poetry' he dramatized the Spaniards' mission as the new chosen people of the Lord, who would avenge the defeat of Portugal on the victorious Moors. His lament 'Por la Pèrdida del Don Sebastian' is rich with Biblical echoes. It deliberately recalls the drowning of Pharaoh's armies in the Red Sea, and repeats phrases from the prophets Isaiah, Jeremiah, and Amos, and from the Book of Daniel. The Lord had used the infidel as an instrument of His divine wrath, and would now raise the Spaniards to the eminence from which His former favourites had fallen. Herrera's visions are grandiose; his mood is one of *Schadenfreude*; he rejoices in the destruction of this rash and Christian king:

> Ai de los que passaron, confiados
> en sus cavallos, i en la muchedumbre
> de sus carros, en ti, Libia desierta;
> i, en su vigor i fuerças engañados,
> no alçaron su esperanza a aquella cumbre
> d'eterna luz; mas con sobervia cierta
> s'ofrecieron la incierta,
> vitoria, i sin bolver a Dios sus ojos,
> con ierto cuello i coraçon ufano
> solo atendieron siempre a los despojos;

> i el Santo d'Israel abrio su mano,
> i los dexò; i cayò en despeñadero,
> el carro, i el cavallo, i cavallero.[1]

But this mood of Herrera's was short-lived. He saw more
Spanish defeats than victories in his lifetime. Between the rout
of Charles V at Algiers, indeed, and Drake's raid on Cadiz his
country shared in only one considerable victory, that of Don
John of Austria over the Turks in the naval battle of Lepanto.
And the Turks quickly recovered their strength; the Low
Countries rose in revolt; the Invincible Armada was over-
come by the English ships and the elements. The Lord had
clearly acquiesced in the defeat of His newly chosen people. In
his elegy 'Al desengaño' ('On disillusion') Herrera reviewed
the rise and fall of nations, all alike overthrown by the swift
wings of Time:

> Veo el tiempo veloz, que s'adelanta
> i derriba con buelo pressuroso
> cuanto el ombre fabrica, i cuanto planta.[2]

He had no hope now that his own country would be exempted
from the fate of Portugal. Though he had once had occasion to
sing a song of praise to the Lord for the victory of Lepanto, his
prognostications were henceforth dark. Addressing the victorious
Turks, he tells them that they have no need to attack again,
since the virtue of Spain has been sapped from within:

> Osadas gentes, duras i sañosas,
> a l'ambicion de cuyo grande pecho
> es pequeño el imperio de las cosas;

[1] Alas for those who perished, trusting in their horses and the multitude
of their chariots, in you, desert Lybia, and deceived by their vigour and
forces, did not raise their hope to that eminence of eternal light; but with a
headstrong pride, promised themselves the uncertain victory, and without
turning their eyes to God, with stiff neck and proud heart, merely continued
to wait for their spoil; and the Holy one of Israel opened His hand and
forsook them; and the chariot fell down the precipice together with the
horse and rider.

[2] I see swift time advancing and overthrowing with hurried wing all that
man builds and all that he establishes.

Teñid en sangre 'l hierro; i el estrecho
passo abrid, ô crueles, a la muerte;
vengad el daño a vuestras onras hecho,
    No bolvais la fiereza i braço fuerte,
i el furor de la ira no vencida,
sobre nuestra desnuda i flaca suerte.
    Que ya la gloria d'el valor perdida
nuestra virtud en ocio se remata;
nuestra virtud, que tanto fue temida.[1]

Losing hope that a golden age might reflower in his own
day, Herrera now relegated it to the distant past. Spain was
truly great, in his eyes, in the days of San Fernando, the
Castilian king who reconquered Córdoba and Seville from the
Moors in the thirteenth century, and whose bones were in
Herrera's day transferred for reburial in the great cathedral
of Seville. His ode commemorating this occasion is the second
of his songs of triumph, and hardly inferior in its plangent
evocation of history to that in which he celebrated the battle
of Lepanto.

The later poets of the Spanish Baroque age, tacitly ad-
mitting the defeat of their country's highest endeavour, rejoiced in the parallel between their own heroic fate and the
destruction of Rome. We have examined Quevedo's sonnets
on the ruins of Rome and on the fallen walls of his own cities
and Rodrigo Caro's is only one of several that mourned for
Itálica, the legionaries' settlement which lay deserted a few
miles from Seville. Saguntum and Numantia, famous for their
heroic resistance to the Carthaginians and the Romans, were
also favourite themes for the poets. Disillusioned by the
present, they proclaimed their sorrowful love for the legendary
past. Death, whose triumphs had been a favourite subject of
fourteenth-century poets, received fresh tribute from Herrera,

[1] Bold people, stern and fierce, to whose great and ambitious courage
ownership of possessions is a small thing; stain your swords with blood, and
open the narrow passage to death, o cruel ones. Revenge the wrong done to
your honour. Do not visit your fierceness and strength and the fury of your
unconquered anger on our naked and weak destiny. For now the glory of
our valour is lost and our virtue perishes in idleness, our virtue which once
was so much feared.

who even in his most triumphant mood had never been wholly on the side of life, and from all his successors up to the last generation of Bocángel and Soto de Rojas, with whom poetry died in Spain, not to be reborn for almost three centuries.

Góngora most eloquently proved his partisanship with death in a number of eloquent funeral sonnets. He had little to say about the destiny of Spain, except indirectly in his panegyric on the royal favourite, the Duke of Lerma—one of his most sustained works, which, however, he broke off when the duke suddenly lost the king's regard. But Góngora had really no sense of the present. Even as he extols the lineage and achievements of his hero, he seems to turn him from a living man into a statue. Choked by the convolutions of the poet's style, Lerma is transformed into a Classical, or rather a mythological, hero. His virtues are superhuman, for his ascent to power, in the poet's eyes, has been entirely disinterested:

> No del impulso conducido vano
> de la ambición, al pie de su gran dueño
> asciende, en cuya poderosa mano
> dos mundos continentes son pequeño;
> alas batiendo luego, al soberano
> sucesor se remonta, en cuyo ceño
> se ríe el alba, Febo reverbera,
> águila generosa de su esfera.[1]

At Philip II's death Lerma was fortunate enough to become the favourite of his son and successor, Philip III, who confirmed with Góngora's evident approval the terms of the treaty of Vervins, by which a long war with France was concluded to Spain's disadvantage:

> Confirmóse la paz, que establecida
> dejó en Vervín Filipo ya Segundo,
> que las últimas sombras de su vida
> puertas de Jano, horror fueron del mundo.

[1] Not led by the vain goad of ambition, he ascends to the foot of his great master, in whose mighty hand two continents or worlds are a trifle; beating his wings, he soon climbs to the next sovereign, on whose brow the dawn smiles and the sun reflects; the generous eagle of his sphere.

De álamos temió entonces vestida
la urna de Erídano profundo
sombras que le hicieron no ligeras,
sus Helíades no, nuestras banderas.[1]

Thus, when we have been briefly informed in the first two
lines that the young king confirmed the old king's treaty our
interest is immediately raised to a higher imaginative level at
which the old king's death is transformed into a mythological
event. The Janus gates which overshadowed the last days of
Philip's life stand quite simply for the state of war, for these
gates of Rome were opened only in times of hostilities; and
war horrifies the whole world. The statement of the next
quatrain, however, is rather more abstruse, since the scene of
the king's death is now removed one stage further from
reality, being compared to the fall of Phaeton who drove the
chariot of his father the sun off its track and was hurled down
by Zeus. Falling into the river Eridanus, which lay on the edge
of the Greek world, facing the Amber Islands, he was mourned
by his sisters, the Heliades, who were transformed into poplars
and wept amber tears. Marvell uses the same image, which
both he and Góngora no doubt drew from a chorus in the
'Hipolytus' of Euripides, to describe the girl's tears in 'The
Nymph complaining for the death of her Fawn':

> The brotherless Heliades
> Melt in such Amber Tears as these.

But the poplars which overhung the death-bed of Philip were
not the sun's sisters; they were *our* banners, drooping in defeat,
and dropping, perhaps, not amber but blood. The return to
reality made in the last half of the last line is most powerful.
Nevertheless, these events remain, as Góngora relates them,

[1] The peace was confirmed which Philip, still the second, had settled at
Vervins, since the last shadows of his life were a Janus gate, a horror for the
world. For he feared the urn [spring] of deep Eridanus, cloaked by poplars,
which threw no light shadows upon him, not his Daughters of the Sun but
our banners.

outside the flux of historical time. He has perpetuated them, as in bronze or marble, so that they exist for ever in the world of art. For Góngora is concerned neither with persons nor with happenings, but only with their reflections in the world of unchanging ideas.

Therefore, as the modern poet Jorge Guillén writes, 'his funeral sonnets have very little to say about death or the person who has died; what bulks large in them is the sepulchre or the tomb. Grief is only a funeral gravity, as the verse . . . rivals the tomb in solidity. In a sonnet on the death of Cardinal Bernardo de Sandoval y Rojas, the deceased does not appear until the eleventh line.'[1] Then he does so only obliquely. What interests Góngora is in the first place the tomb, and in the final tercet the coat-of-arms of the dead man that is carved and painted on it:

> Esta que admiras fábrica, este prima
> pompa de la escultura, oh caminante,
> en pórfidos rebeldes al diamante,
> en metales mordidos de la lima
>
> tierra sella que tierra nunca oprima;
> si ignoras cúya, el pie enfrena ignorante,
> y esta inscripción consulta, que elegante
> informa bronces, mármoles anima.
>
> Generosa piedad urnas hoy bellas
> con majestad vincula, con decoro,
> a las heroicas ya cenizas santas
>
> de los que, a un campo de oro cinco estrellas
> dejando azules, con mejores plantas
> en campo azul estrellas pisan de oro.[2]

---

[1] See *Language and Poetry*, p. 39.

[2] This fabric on which you gaze, this prime glory of sculpture, O traveller, of porphyry too hard for the diamond, and metal incised with the file, seals up earth [the corpse] which may the earth never oppress; if you do not know whose earth, stay your ignorant foot and study this inscription, which elegantly makes bronze speak and calls marble to life. Liberal piety links urns now beautiful with majesty, with propriety, to the heroic and now sacred ashes of those who, leaving five blue stars on a field of gold, with better feet tread golden stars on a blue field.

Here is monumentality without movement. The spectator is told to pause; the dead cardinal himself has no motion; he is merely at one with his ancestors, treading—a favourite word of Góngora's which has its own weight—the golden stars.

If Góngora wishes to denote movement he does so in a monumental way, by showing a motionless bird on the point of taking flight. Galatea, bending over Acis, who pretends to sleep, is compared in the 'Fábula de Polifemo y Galatea' to a stooping eagle:

> no el ave reina, no el fragoso nido
> corona inmóvil, mientras no desciende
> —rayo con plumas—al milano pollo
> que la eminencia abriga de un escollo.[1]

Thus Góngora freezes instability into a guise of 'monumental stillness'. Galatea for ever bends over her lover. The rock which the giant Polyphemus afterwards hurls at Acis no sooner strikes him than it becomes his tomb. It does not fall through the air. We merely see it at the end of its flight, frozen into perpetual immobility:

> Con vïolencia desgajó infinita
> la mayor punta de la excelsa roca,
> que al joven, sobre quien la precipita,
> urna es mucha, pirámide no poca.[2]

The tomb of Acis in some sense represents the burial place of Spain's poetic greatness. True, the 'Soledades' were still to

[1] The eagle, queen of the other birds, does not remain so motionless as she crowns her inaccessible nest still not descending—like a winged lightning —on the young kite, who is hidden by the crest of a crag. (Translation from prose adaptation by Dámaso Alonso, *Góngora y el 'Polifemo'*, p. 409.)

[2] With an enormous effort Polyphemus wrenched the topmost point from the lofty crag, which served the youth on whom he hurled it as an urn too large to hold his remains, a funeral pyramid of some size. (Translation from ibid., p. 498.) See Guillén, op. cit., p. 54.

be written. But the youth who incarnated the fresh style that Garcilaso had initiated was, once Góngora reached his prime, soon crushed by the one-eyed Polyphemus of Baroque ingenuity. The garlands withered on his 'funeral pyramid'; or would have withered had not Góngora and his successors cast them in a bronze which remained smooth and polished if no longer green.

In France, too, burnished bronze replaced the living green of Ronsard's and du Bellay's style. The modelling was more classical and correct; the symmetrical couplet of François de Malherbe and his successors cannot be compared with the antithetical and paradoxical manner ('urna es mucha, pirámide no poco)' of the Gongorists. Nor was France defeated in the struggle for cultural and imperial supremacy until the next century. In welcoming Henry IV's new queen, Marie de Medicis, to France, Malherbe congratulated the king on having humbled the Spaniards, with whom he had made that peace at Vervins which had lifted the last shadows from the death-bed of Philip II, and also on having calmed the troubles of the religious wars:

> Qu'il lui suffise que l'Espagne,
> Réduite par tant de combats
> A ne l'oser voir en campagne,
> A mis l'ire et les armes bas;
> Qu'il ne provoque point l'envie
> Du mauvais sort contre sa vie;
> Et puisque, selon son dessein,
> Il a rendu nos troubles calmes,
> S'il veut d'avantage de palmes,
> Qu'il les acquiert en votre sein.[1]

Malherbe had abandoned the Marinist style in which he had written his first important poem, 'Les Larmes de Saint-

[1] Let him be satisfied that Spain, beaten in so many battles that she no longer dares to face him in the field, has abated her fury and laid down her arms; that he no longer arouses the envy of adverse fate against his life; and since, according to his plan, he has now calmed our troubles, if he wants any more laurels, he may now acquire them in your breast.

Pierre'. The language of his panegyric on the new queen is regular, and, by Baroque standards, flat. If it aims at grandeur its endeavour is for a sustained elevation, devoid of special embellishments. France was just at the beginnings of her advance to political and cultural supremacy. A quarter of a century later, when Henry was dead, and his son Louis XIII was destroying the last remnants of Huguenot power in an endeavour for national and religious unity like that of Spain, Malherbe attempted a more ambitious manner. Welcoming the king home from a petty campaign against the fortress of La Rochelle and a half-hearted English expedition which had come to its aid, he adopted a hectoring style, with Biblical echoes, which is reminiscent of Herrera's though less extravagant in language and less incantatory. The incident is baroquely disproportionate. But it is translated into severely Classical terms. The young king, like another Jupiter, is reseated on his throne by the virgin Victory, who has aided his minister Richelieu to overthrow the Rochelois, here represented by the Titans of Greek myth:

> Déjà de tous côtés s'avançaient les approches;
> Içi courait Mimas; là Typhon se battait;
> Et là suait Euryte à détacher les roches
>   Qu'Encélade jetait.
> À peine cette Vierge eut l'affaire embrassée,
> Qu'aussitôt Jupiter en son trône remis,
> Vit selon son désir la tempête cessée,
>   Et n'eut plus d'ennemis.
> Ces colosses d'orgueil furent tous mis en poudre,
> Et tous couverts des monts qu'ils avaient arrachés:
> Phlègre, qui les reçut, pue encore la foudre
>   Dont ils furent touchés.[1]

[1] Already from all sides the attackers advanced; there Mimas ran; there Typhon fought; and there Eurytus sweated to uproot the rocks which Enceladus threw. Scarcely had that virgin [Victory] taken up their cause than straightway Jupiter, replaced on his throne, saw the storm cease as he desired, and had no more enemies. Those giants of pride were all pulverized and all covered by the mountains they had uprooted. Phlegra, which received them, still stinks of the thunderbolt with which they were struck.

There is a curious disproportion between the poem and its
imagery. Treating a similar subject, Don Juan's victory at
Lepanto, Herrera put it in the broad setting of the age-old
contest between east and west, in Biblical, Classical, Mediaeval, and Modern times. Like his lament over the defeat of
Don Sebastião, it recalls the rhythms of the Hebrew Psalms
and the Prophets. Malherbe, on the other hand, rejecting the
metaphorical style that he had used as a young man, finds
grandeur in measured verse and a slow development of
imagery. Where Góngora would have passed from a comparison with the Titans to another and yet another in verse
after verse, Malherbe piles Pelion on Ossa rock by rock. The
deliberate calm of his

. . . tous couverts des monts qu'ils avaient arrachés

contrasts strangely with the single compressed phrase with
which Góngora describes the crushing and entombment of
Acis. Góngora's movement is so swift that all appears motionless. Herrera's sweep and excitement are such that the engagement he celebrates seems to be one in an endless battle that
began in the first days of history. All is pulsing movement.
Malherbe, in contrast to both, tries to lend Roman dignity to
what is essentially an unimportant incident. Moreover, his
imagery is no more organic to the poem than a Roman toga
to the statue of a seventeenth-century statesman.

Louis XIII is more fittingly, because more exaggeratedly,
lauded by the Italian Marinist Claudio Achillini at the next
stage of his career when, having conquered La Rochelle, he
came to fight a short campaign in Italy. The opening has the
true Baroque excess of an aria by Alessandro Scarlatti or the
early Handel:

> Sudate, o fochi, a preparar metalli,
> e voi, ferri vitali, itene pronti,
> ite di Paro a sviscerare i monti
> per innalzar colossi al Re de' Galli.

Vinse l'invitta rocca e de' vassalli
spezzò gli orgogli a le rubelle fronti,
e machinando inusitati ponti
diè fuga ai mari e gli converse in valli.[1]

The account of the conquest of La Rochelle is so fore-shortened as to be legendary. The poem bears only the slightest relation to its ostensible subject. Even as the bronze and marble statue of Louis XIII, which Achillini demands, will idealize out of all recognition the face and bearing of its subject, so this sonnet, far from following the actual events, raises to a quintessential dignity happenings which in themselves contained little that was either admirable or heroic. The voyages of da Gama, narrated by Camões, and the victory of Lepanto, celebrated by Herrera, were events on the scale of history. The conquest of La Rochelle and Louis' descent into Italy were on a comparatively petty scale; and the deflection of a few watercourses, no doubt a good job of engineering, remains a little absurd even when compressed by Achillini into a couple of slightly ambiguous lines. The purpose of his complimentary sonnet, however, is not to exalt history but art. Malherbe purports to believe in his classical comparison between the citizen armies of the Huguenots and the Titans of old. Achillini reminds Louis that it is only in the form of a work of art—a marble statue crowned with bronze laurels—that he will survive in human memory as one greater than Caesar, since his Italian campaign was so brief that

. . . se Cesare venne e vide e vinse,
venne, vinse e non vide il gran Luigi.[2]

Historical events were becoming absurd. Now that the

[1] Sweat, O fires, to prepare metals, and you, living iron [i.e. the tools which cut marble], depart quickly, go to disembowel the mountains of Paros, to erect great statues to the King of Gaul. He conquered the unvanquished rock [La Rochelle] and broke the pride on the rebel brows of his vassals, and building unheard-of bridges, put the seas to flight and turned them into valleys.

[2] If Caesar came, saw and conquered, the great Louis came, conquered and did not see.

bitter and devastating civil wars were over, the field was open for the would-be Caesars, who collected thrones and provinces as their contemporaries, the India merchants, bankers, and bill-brokers, collected houses, furniture, and other valuables. Marvell's 'Last Instructions to a Painter' describe an incident in one of these petty wars of commercial rivalry—the Dutch raid on the Medway of 1666, in which the neglected English fleet was destroyed at anchor. No national enmity was involved, and though some lives were no doubt lost, nothing was done that could not quickly be remedied with the next change of alliance. Marvell could therefore take a parodic, mock-heroic view of these events at Sheerness. He shows the old Dutch admiral Ruyter cocking a senile eye at the bathing nymphs as he leads up the Thames estuary a fleet as miniature as if it were painted on the vacant corner of a chart:

> Their streaming silks play through the weather fair,
> And with inveigling Colours Court the Air.
> While the red Flags breathe on their Top-masts high
> Terrour and War, but want an enemy.

Marvell lightly moves on to describe a comic Neptune who heaves their stranded ships off the banks and draw a conventional Aeolus who 'puffs them along', and then to develop an Homeric simile, compared with which Malherbe's genteel Classicism appears ponderously unclassical:

> So have I seen, in April's bud, arise
> A Fleet of Clouds, sailing along the Skies:
> The liquid Region with their Squadrons fill'd
> The airy Sterne the Sun behind does guild;
> And gentle Gales them steer, and Heaven drives,
> When, all on sudden, their calm bosome rives
> With Thunder and Lightning from each armed Cloud;
> Shepherds themselves in vain in bushes shroud.
> Such up the stream the Belgick Navy glides,
> And at Sheerness unloads its stormy sides.

By this miniature presentation Marvell gives the events

of 1666 their due proportion. In his 'Horatian Ode upon
Cromwell's Return from Ireland' he places in an equally just
historical retrospect an event of greater consequence—the
execution of Charles I, against whom he had reluctantly taken
sides. His praise is equally apportioned between the 'Royal
Actor' and the 'Man',

> Who, from his private gardens, where
> He lived reserved and austere,
> As if his highest plot
> To plant the Bergamot,
> Could by industrious valour climbe
> To ruine the great Work of Time,
>   And cast the Kingdome old
>   Into another mold.

Marvell sees the contrast between the two men in personal
terms, but also, by a just Classical parallel, in its context as a
necessary stage in the growth of English freedom. His historical
penetration is as remarkable as the economy of the famous
verses in which he praises Charles's conduct on the scaffold:

> He nothing common did or mean
> Upon that memorable scene:
>   But with his keener Eye
>   The Axes edge did try:
> Nor call'd the Gods with vulgar spight
> To vindicate his helpless Right,
>   But bow'd his comely Head,
>   Down as upon a Bed.
> This was that memorable Hour
> Which first assur'd the forced Pow'r.
>   So when they did design
>   The Capitol's first Line,
> A bleeding Head where they begun,
> Did fright the Architects to run;
>   And yet in that the State
>   Foresaw its happy Fate.

There are only two similes in this passage, one short and the other more extended, the first visual and the second intellectual or historical. Yet Marvell's texture is extremely rich. He even makes a play on the Latin word *acies*, in its double-meaning of 'eyesight' and 'keen edge', that has been noted by Professor Empson.[1] His compression, indeed, is far more Classical than Malherbe's. Wishing to stress the superhuman majesty of Henry IV, the French poet observes, with quite un-Horatian prolixity, in his 'Vers Funèbres', how astonishing it is that the king should suffer the common fate of death:

> Henri, ce grand Henri, que les soins de nature
> Avaient fait un miracle aux yeux de l'univers,
> Comme un homme vulgaire est dans la sépulture
> A la merci des vers.[2]

Malherbe is not at his best as an historical poet. He lacks perspective and, when he prophesies, his guess is wrong.

Certainly there is not even a tinge of probability in that passage in his poem of welcome to Marie de Médicis—it occurs a little before the passage referring to the treaty of Vervins—in which he prognosticates the conquest of Turkey by her infant son, who was afterwards Louis XIII:

> Oh! combien lors aura de veuves
> La gent qui porte le turban!
> Que de sang rougira les fleuves
> Qui lavent les pieds du Liban!
> Que le Bosphore en ses deux rives
> Aura de Sultanes captives!
> Et que de mères à Memphis,
> En pleurant diront la vaillance
> De son courage et de sa lance,
> Aux funérailles de leurs fils![3]

[1] See *Seven Types of Ambiguity*, p. 166.

[2] Henry, that great Henry, whom the work of nature had made a miracle in the eyes of the universe, like a common man, is in the tomb, at the mercy of the worms.

[3] Oh, how many widows will they then have, the people who wear the turban! How much blood will redden the rivers which wash the feet of

The imagery is flat and the language unconvincing. The armour of a latter-day crusader was no more suitable to a seventeenth-century king than the toga of a Caesar. But that realism which is to be found in the poetry of the charnel-house and of profane love failed to influence the writing of compliments to the living great and epitaphs on the illustrious dead.

Even Quevedo was not ashamed to offer gross adulation to the Spanish royal family. It is hard to associate the Infanta and nun Margarita of Austria, whose glorious tomb he celebrated in a sonnet, with her long-faced, blubber-lipped Habsburg relatives who stare vacantly and proudly down from Velázquez' portraits. One wonders about the reality of the plain serge and modest veil, and gasps at the comparison with St Francis:

> ¡ Oh, cuán cesáreas venas, cuán sagradas
> frentes se coronaron con tu velo!
> Y espléndido el sayal, venció en el suelo
> púrpura tiria y minas de oro hiladas.
>   La silla más excelsa, más gloriosa,
> que perdió el serafín amotinado
> premió a Francisco la humildad; y hoy osa
>   la tierra, émula al cielo, en alto grado
> premiarle con la frente más preciosa
> que imperiales coronas han cercado.[1]

Velázquez represented the Habsburgs better, and with greater kindness. For the evident disproportion between the real princess and Quevedo's saintly caricature is as revealing and, in effect, as satirical as a portrait by that more evident despiser of royalty Francisco Goya.

Lebanon! How many Sultanas will the two shores of the Bosphorus yield as prisoners! And how many mothers at Memphis will tell with tears, at the funerals of their sons, of his prowess and the strength of his lance!

[1] Oh, how many Caesarian veins, how many holy foreheads have been crowned with your veil! And the splendid serge has conquered Tyrian purple and mines of woven gold on the earth. The highest and most glorious throne forfeited by the rebellious seraphim was the reward for Francis' humility; and now earth, rivalling heaven, dares to reward it most highly with the most precious brow that has been encircled by imperial crowns.

In the seventeenth century, however, satire was timid in its direct attacks on those in power. Nicolas Boileau-Despreaux, in his 'Epître IV', modestly followed the progress of his royal master through Holland, noting the rebarbative names of the villages which resisted him, and wishing that the king would direct his campaigns into lands richer in high-sounding places. He even ground out a stiff ode to Louis in which he celebrated the capture of Namur.

It was left to Protestant England, by means of the mock-heroic, to prick the bladder of military prowess and renown, which poets were free to do, at least in retrospect, once the Civil Wars were concluded and some freedom of speech and comment guaranteed. Samuel Butler, who as a Cavalier had emerged on the winning side, could poke unlimited fun not only at the defeated factions but at the whole composition of middle-class society. His weakness was that he made too facile use of his model *Don Quixote*. Failing to realize that Cervantes was a serious critic of illusions of whatever kind, and that his knight represented the powers of the imagination, while Sancho just as solidly stood for those of peasant intuition, Butler made his knight Hudibras and his squire Ralph mere facetious entertainers. By their lack of Baroque extravagance they show that though Classicism had not yet triumphed in England as it had in France, the Baroque age was ending there also. Nothing more trenchant than a rather obtuse common sense obtained in Butler's world, in which a certain nonconformist, who kept bears at Southwark and appears to have been a quack-doctor, is caricatured as the bear-leader Orsin:

> Thus virtuous Orsin was endued
> With learning, conduct, fortitude,
> Incomparable: and as the prince
> Of poets, Homer, sung long since,
> A skilful leech is better far
> Than half a hundred men of war;
> So he appear'd, and by his skill,
> No less than dint of sword, could kill.

Butler scores his superficial points as readily at the expense of poetry, here personified in Homer, as against war, heroism, religious theory, and political faction.

It was, in general, poetry itself that presented the readiest target to the disillusioned in the late seventeenth century. The poets were most violent against one another. Malherbe slashed the verses of Ronsard and Desportes; and Quevedo, Jáuregui, and Lope attacked Góngora's style with all the bitterness of personal rancour. Malherbe's attacks on his fore-runners and contemporaries were based on matters of poetic practice. But the vast palaces of art erected by the poets of the High Baroque, as a refuge from the cold winds of war and religious doubt, now came under general attack. The world was passing into an age of prose. So, abdicating the extreme claims of the imagination, the poets after 1660 turned their attention either to petty matters which could be recorded by a neat turn of phrase or to broad satire. In either case there was a renunciation of the Baroque anxiety. Neither the précieux poetry of Tristan l'Hermite nor the satire of Butler, Dryden, and Boileau contains any great charge of emotion. The old Baroque imagery is used by the former, but only as for decorative effect. The theme of the macabre has been ren-dered harmless in such a sonnet as 'À des Cimetières', in which Tristan tritely concludes that his lady's unkindness is far more lethal than any thought of death:

> Tombeaux, pâles témoins de la rigueur du Sort
> Où je viens en secret entretenir la Mort
> D'un amour que je vois si mal recompensée.
>
> Vous donnez de la crainte et de l'horreur à tous;
> Mais le plus doux objet qui s'offre à ma pensée
> Est beaucoup plus funeste et plus triste que vous.[1]

Mme de Mourgues, in quoting this poem and developing her analysis of Preciosity,[2] argues that whereas the purely

[1] Tombs, pale witnesses of the harshness of Fate, to which I secretly resort to dwell on the death of a love that I see so ill rewarded, you inspire fear and horror in all. But the sweet object who comes to my thoughts is much more desolating and mournful than you.

[2] Op. cit., pp. 134–6.

Baroque poets were unaware of the fantastic nature of their distorted universe, 'the discrepancy between the larger field of actual experience and the limited précieux world is the basic principle on which this kind of poetry rests'.

The poet will not express his consciousness of this. If he did so he might have to argue it out in the Metaphysical manner. So poetry has become for him and his reader a game of make-believe, in which both agree to suspend their disbelief. The lady is not supposed to accept the statement that her unkindness is worse than death as literally true. Everyone is aware that the poetic coinage has been devalued, and that such words as 'crainte', 'horreur', and 'funeste' have no longer their full worth as currency. In fact the poet's disillusion with the great emotions of love, heroism, and art is as truly expressed in this petty coinage of preciosity as by the preposterous adulations of Quevedo, or in the more commonsensical field of satire. Not till the Romantic age will poets again attempt to speak from the depths of their hearts.

James Shirley, the last of the Jacobean dramatists, writing in the year before the Restoration in a Baroque style that was already touched by preciosity, expressed the final resignation of the heroic poet before the inevitability of a swift oblivion in which he and his deeds, his thoughts and his fame, would alike perish:

> The glories of our blood and state,
> 　　Are shadows, not substantial things,
> There is no armour against fate,
> 　　Death lays his icy hand on Kings
> 　　　　　Scepter and Crown,
> 　　　　　Must tumble down,
> And in the dust be equal made,
> With the poor crooked sithe and spade.
>
> Some men with swords may reap the field,
> 　　And plant fresh laurels where they kill,
> But their strong nerves at last must yield,
> 　　They tame but one another still;

> Early or late,
> They stoop to fate,
> And must give up their murmuring breath,
> When they pale Captives creep to death.
>
> The Garlands wither on your brow,
>   Then boast no more your mighty deeds,
> Upon death's purple altar now,
>   See where the Victor-victim bleeds,
>   Your heads must come,
>   To the cold Tomb;
> Onely the actions of the just
> Smell sweet, and blossom in their dust.

The defeat which had been heroic in the case of Don Sebastião, slaughtered by the Moors, was now seen as the lot of every ambitious ruler and of every would-be conqueror. Outward action was, as Calderón expressed it in his drama 'La vida es sueño', an illusion; one dreamt that one was awake, and one likewise dreamt that one was dreaming. Not only was glory insubstantial in Shirley's eyes but he knew that the pursuit of it led to nothing but a mutual attrition:

> They tame but one another still.

Moreover, his statement was made objectively and with pity. His verse runs smoothly; it is free from the broken rhythms of Sponde and Chassignet, and even of Donne, who all struggled against the need for resignation. Nor does Shirley surrender to melancholy, as Tristan does in his ghost-haunted cemetery. Victor is victim, and laurels are no sooner planted than they wither. 'Only the actions of the just', he concludes, survive. The great empire-building panorama with which Camões ushered in the Baroque age has shrunk to the tiny field of personal rectitude. But, who, at the end of the long Civil War, were to be called 'the just'? Was it those who had been successful, and by a compromise with the more moderate members of the defeated party had attained precarious power? Again, who among the poets would claim that his garlands were untarnished? For an age in which the martial garlands had first begun to wither saw, towards the end, no greater freshness in the poet's bays. All claims to any greatness except that of mere station were now called into question. For who among the poets could lay claim to that rectitude which was lacking in the soldiers and statesmen? The passionate Crashaw, who died in exile, cantankerously attacking the immoralities of the Roman Church to which he had attached himself? The detached Marvell, a civil servant in one government and a member of Parliament in the next? Or the religious conformer Dryden, who changed his Church as he changed his politics? Should a man be considered just because he subscribed to a certain theology, and irrespective of his private actions? It is the religious aspects of Baroque poetry that we must now examine in our last two chapters.

8

The dictatorship of the scribes

THE Renaissance had freed the arts and sciences from the domination of theology. The Counter-Reformation, though acknowledging the advance of scholarship which the New Learning had brought, firmly subordinated it, nevertheless, to a new theological domination. The themes of poetry, in the entirely Catholic southern countries, were perhaps extended; the poet's individual judgement was, however, curtailed. To compare Milton's freedom to relate the myth of the Fall in his own way with Calderón's strict treatment of theological propositions in his *Autos sacramentales* is to realize, at a single glance, the gulf that had now opened between the northern and the Mediterranean lands.

It is not that fine poetry cannot be written without a breach with religious orthodoxy. Milton himself, in his ode 'On the Morning of Christ's Nativity', a poem which contains more Baroque imagery than any of his others, first sees the Birth as promising, in pagan fashion, the return of the golden age:

> Ring out ye Crystall sphears,
> Once bless our human ears,
>   (if ye have power to touch our senses so)
> And let your silver chime
> Move in melodious time;
>   And let the Base of Heav'ns deep Organ blow,
> And with your ninefold harmony
> Make up full consort to th' Angelike symphony.

> For if such holy Song
> Enwrap our fancy long,
>   Time will run back, and fetch the age of gold,
> And speckl'd vanity
> Will sicken soon and die,
>   And leprous sin will melt from earthly mould,
> And Hell it self will pass away,
> And leave her dolorous mansions to the peering day.

The imagery is not Christian. Milton's harmony is the Pythagorean music of the spheres; and its use at this moment is particularly significant. For though the Baroque age began with a growing affinity between poetry and the visual, predominance among the arts was now, as has already been suggested, swinging over towards music. Already the opera was absorbing talents which would previously have been given to the drama; Calderón himself was writing the texts for romantic musical comedies. From Monteverdi's 'Orfeo' to the 'full consort' of Bach and Handel, music advanced while the other arts merely developed themes that had already been stated by the beginning of the seventeenth century. Góngora perfects an art that is founded on that of his forerunners. Vergil, Theocritus, Ariosto, Sannazzaro—all have contributed to the texture of the 'Soledades'. Bach, on the other hand, though resuming the manners of his immediate predecessors, both German and Italian, transformed their inheritance into something immeasurably greater than Schütz, Buxtehude, Telemann, Vivaldi, or Couperin could have dreamt of. Music ceased to be a light entertainment or an accompaniment to worship; it was now capable of expressing the greatest experience in its own medium. It was now largely independent of the often trivial words which the poets gave to its singers.

Poetry, on the other hand, suffered from restriction of thought. Théophile de Viau, for example, was persecuted for making platonic statements which were no more dangerous than Milton had made in the introduction to his Nativity Ode, where he had pictured the earth as a living creature, the lover of the sun. Milton, however, firmly rejected this momentary vision of the world's redemption and the return of the golden age as a result of the Birth alone, and returned in the next verse to the Crucifixion and the Last Judgement:

> But wisest Fate sayes no,
> This must not yet be so,
> The Babe lies yet in smiling Infancy
> That on that bitter cross
> Must redeem our loss;
> So both himself and us to glorifie:
> Yet first to those ychain'd in sleep,
> The wakeful trump of doom must thunder through
> the deep.

This pagan reference to Fate as the director of the whole drama, and to the age of gold as an historical state from which man had fallen, is firmly subordinated to the Christian story. The Counter-Reformation retained all the resources of Classical mythology, upon which the Renaissance had drawn, but relegated them to the sphere of imagery, or sometimes to 'typology', the pagan god or hero being allowed to represent some aspect of the true deity. Even in the Catholic south the pagan deities continued to illustrate and adorn. Jupiter could stand for God the Father in his creative or commanding aspects; and a pagan Fate appears for Fontanella, as for Milton, as the final arbitress in his sonnet 'Meditazione della sua morte':

> Verrà la Parca, e di pallor gelato
> l'insegna spanderà sopra il mio volto,
> e dentro un letto di miserie accolto
> con angoscia trarrò l'ultimo fiato.[1]

But Fontanella quickly turns to contemplate the more

---

[1] Fate will come and with icy pallor spread her banner over my face, and lying in anguish on a bed of misery I shall draw my last breath.

Christian figures of his 'harsh adversary', the devil, and the Virgin,

>   alta reina,
> da quell' empiree e luminose squadre[1]

whom he implores to receive him into her maternal bosom.

The Virgin and the Magdalene, favourite subjects of the Baroque painters, are treated with varying degrees of contrived sensuality by the Catholic poets of the time. Crashaw savours the tears of the Penitent to their last Metaphysical drop. For in 'The Weeper' he is concerned not with the Magdalene's character or story, nor with her conversion from sinner to saint, but solely with the flowing of her eyes, upon which he builds a succession of conceits:

> Does thy day-starre rise?
> Still thy starres do fall and fall.
> Does day close his eyes?
> Still the Fountain weeps for all.
> Let night or day doe what they will,
> Thou hast thy task; thou weepest still.

Fontanella, in his sonnet on the Magdalene, remembers her vanity as well as her tears, and somewhat strangely transforms her in his last line into the chaste huntress:

> Così, presso una limpida fontana,
> de le lagrime sue purgando l'alma
> ov'era Citerea, sembra Diana.[2]

To Crashaw, the Magdalene appears to weep for the sins of the world, to Fontanella only for her own, and to Marino, who devoted a long poem to Titian's portrait of the Penitent (now in the Pitti Palace), considering her feature by feature— eyes, tears, hair, mouth, hand—she seems

[1] Exalted queen of those heavenly and shining squadrons.
[2] Thus, beside a limpid spring, purging her soul with her tears, where she was Cytherea, she seems like Diana.

Questa, che 'n atto supplice e pentita
se stessa aflige in solitaria cella,
e de la prima età fresca e fiorita
piange le colpe, in un dolente e bella . . .[1]

The Magdalene has, in fact, become, with no apparent
shock to theology, a female counterpart of the Redeemer. 'Sad
and beautiful at once', she has taken upon herself the sins of
carnality, and by renouncing them has somehow succeeded
in reintroducing the Renaissance glories of the flesh into the
kingdom of heaven. For no Baroque painter ever represented
her as other than a beautiful and sensually desirable woman,
more attractive in her tears than in her previously unapproach-
able pride.

Another object of the Baroque poet and painter's adulation,
Santa Teresa of Ávila, did not so readily adapt herself to the
ideal of a woman saint which the age had adopted. Only with
great difficulty can one reconcile the picture of the active
reformer and struggling visionary which Teresa draws in her
autobiography with the 'sweet incendiary' invoked by Crashaw
in 'The Flaming Heart'. No adjective could be more un-
suitable for that scourge of her sentimental 'daughters' than
'sweet'.

The cult of individual saints reveals only one side of the
Baroque poet's sensual pietism. The three books of 'Théorèmes
spirituels' (spiritual propositions or subjects of contemplation)
by the Provençal magistrate Jean de la Ceppède attempt to
tell the story of the Passion, Death, and Resurrection of
Christ. In some five hundred sonnets he covers the whole
Biblical narrative, pausing at intervals to dwell on any point
that is baffling to the intellect, illuminating each incident with
'figures' or parallels drawn from the Old Testament, and
enriching it with symbolism taken from astrology, or based on
a theory of colours which anticipates the 'Correspondences' of
Baudelaire. La Ceppède is master of a more vigorous rhetoric

[1] She who by the practice of suppliance and repentence punishes herself
in her solitary cell and weeps for the sins of her fresh and flowering prime,
sad and beautiful at once.

than the Marinists. He is more single-minded than any of his Spanish or French contemporaries. Flamboyant, hyperbolical, and at times tasteless, even at his most intellectual he is seldom flat in the manner of Du Bartas. Though the New Testament drama possesses him like a nightmare, in which each moment is prolonged beyond its time, and every object is larger than it would be in the waking world, he still makes use of incidents from profane literature, from mythology, and from Nature, to heighten his melodramatic effects. The opening of the second sonnet, which he devotes with characteristic slow-motion to the insults which Christ suffered at the hands of Caiphas, shows the feverish power with which La Ceppède extracted from the smallest material hint the maximum of pathos:

> Le beau Printemps n'a point tant de feuillages verts,
> L'Hiver tant de glaçons, l'Été tant de javelles,
> Que durant cette nuit le Roi de l'Univers
> Souffre d'indignités et de peines nouvelles,
>   Constant observateur de ses lois éternelles,
> Il pâtit sans jamais rabrouer ces pervers.
> Tandis les tons secrets des trompes paternelles
> (Non encor entendus) sont ores découverts.[1]

La Ceppède is so prone to bring out all the trumpets of the divine orchestra that he has hardly any resources left for a passage that demands greater weight in which he contemplates Christ after the scourging and crowning with thorns. Here he rises to even more grand and hectic chords:

> Voici l'Homme, ô mes yeux, quel objet déplorable!
> La honte, le veiller, la faute d'aliment,
> Les douleurs, et le sang perdu si largement
> L'ont bien tant déformé qu'il n'est plus désirable.

[1] Fair spring has not so many green leaves, nor winter so many icicles, nor summer so many sheaves as the fresh tortures and indignities that the King of the Universe suffered that night. Strict observer of his eternal laws, he suffers without even scolding those wretches. Meanwhile, the secret music of his father's trumpets (never heard before) is now revealed.

Ces cheveux (l'ornement de son chef vénérable)
Sanglantés, hérissés, par ce couronnement,
Embrouillés dans ces joncs, servent d'indignement
A son tête ulceré d'une haie exécrable.

Ces yeux (tantôt si beaux) rebattus, renfoncés,
Resalis, sont hélas! deux Soleils éclipsés,
Le coral de sa bouche est ores jaune-pâle.

Les roses, et les lis de son teint sont flétris:
Le reste de son Corps est de couleur d'Opale,
Tant de la tête aux pieds ses membres sont meurtris.[1]

The accent on bodily pain and disfigurement unites La
Ceppède with the charnel-house poets, his contemporaries in
his own country and in Germany. The 'roses and lilies' of the
Saviour's complexion, on the other hand, and the coral of His
lips remind us rather of the more sensual and peaceful world
of Crashaw, Marino, and Fontanella. Guido Reni, the flesh
of whose dead Christ is the same 'couleur d'opale', was the
inhabitant of an imaginative world similar to this obscure
Provençal gentleman's.

The 'Théorèmes' were too violent and ill-finished to gain
popularity even in their own day. Malherbe wrote a
complimentary sonnet on the occasion of their publication,
but perhaps valued the man more than the poet. Certainly
his poetry violated all the rules of classical propriety which
Malherbe established and by which other poets soon came to
be judged. Lately some of these five hundred sonnets have been
included in anthologies, where they are presented as the
French counterpart to such English Metaphysical poetry as
Donne's 'Divine Sonnets'. In fact, however, the comparison is
not a true one, since, unlike Donne, La Ceppède does not

[1] Ecce homo, o my eyes, what a piteous object; humiliation, sleeplessness, lack of food, pain and a great loss of blood have so disfigured him that
he is no longer desirable. That hair (the adornment of his venerable head),
bloodstained, dishevelled by that crowning, tangled in those reeds, is an
insult to his skull wounded by horrible thorns. Those eyes, once so beautiful,
bruised, battered and blackened, are, alas, two eclipsed suns, the coral of his
lips is now pale yellow. The roses and lilies of his complexion have withered,
the rest of his body is the colour of opal, so bruised are his limbs from head
to foot.

bring his own religious situation into his sonnets. At most he demands to be saved from fear by election as one of God's fold:

> Les marqués de ton coin n'eurent jadis à craindre;
> Je ne craindrai non plus, s'il te plaît de t'empreindre
> Par le burin d'amour sur le roc de mon cœur.[1]

But fear is always present. It is vouched for by the excited hyperbole which pervades the whole of the 'Théorèmes'. Even his unquestioning acceptance of the New Testament and of its prefiguration in the Old did not bring La Ceppède the confidence he needed. Somewhere in the 'mysteries' that he expounded lay a secret menace, some possibility of damnation, against which he could not comfort himself with the assurance that death had not the power to hurt him for long:

> Ce n'est que pour bien peu que le trépas nous nuit:
> Tout homme après la mort une autre fois respire.
> Cette aube renaissante est la mort de la nuit.[2]

Other French poets of La Ceppède's time were affirmative not only, as he was, in their matter, but also in their manner. Indeed they seem to have closer affinities with Milton than with the Marinists and the charnel-house poets. Du Bois Hus, in particular, whose poem 'La Nuit des Nuits' celebrates Christmas Eve and Christmas Day, seems to have read and even imitated the ode 'On the Morning of Christ's Nativity'. Of du Bois Hus's other work nothing is known, nor does there exist any information concerning his life. In 1640 he published his single poem to which he gave the sub-title 'La Naissance des deux Dauphins du Ciel et de la Terre', thus relating it to the birth two years earlier of the Dauphin, who was afterwards to

[1] Those marked with your die had nothing to fear. I will not fear either if it will please you to cut yourself with the graver of love on the rock of my heart.

[2] It is only for a short time that death hurts us. Every man after death breathes again. This reborn dawn is the death of night.

be Louis XIV. His language, however, though equally lyrical, was more conventionally poetic than Milton's. His adjectives are more predictable in the verse which he devotes to the silence of the night before the birth than that in Milton's on the same theme. His first line has a Miltonic impact, which he dissipates by the conventionality of the next:

> Le Silence vêtu de noir,
> Retournant faire son devoir,
> Vole sur la mer et la terre,
> Et l'Océan joyeux de sa tranquillité
> Est un liquide verre
> Où la face du ciel imprime sa beauté.[1]

Though Du Bois Hus in his best verses achieves a music almost equal to Milton's, there is a more magical evocation of silence in the English poet's lines:

> The Windes with wonder whist,
> Smoothly the waters kist,
> Whispering new joys to the milde Ocean,

and this is achieved not solely by a greater originality of language but by the hushing assonance of repeated *w* and *wh* sounds. Du Bois Hus achieves his effect rather by the use of a Baroque landscape between two lights, with which he arouses a mood of expectation. He makes no religious statement, and finds neither new words nor images with which to draw his landscape. Yet, by conveying a sense of awe, he achieves an almost Wordsworthian numinosity, rare in French poetry.

Many French poets of the period after the religious wars turned their attention to imitating and translating the Psalms, a convention in which they could express their rejoicing in Nature, and could praise God with conventional piety or even with rich ecstasy. François de Malherbe, whose controlled and

---

[1] Black-cloaked silence, returning to its task, glides over sea and earth, and the Ocean, rejoicing in its quiet, is a liquid glass on which the face of the sky imprints its beauty.

formal language was to provide the model for poets of the post-Baroque age, seldom rises above the former state. He seems to address his maker in the mood of a Laureate who, while willing to confess his shortcomings, is at the same time very conscious of his merits. His paraphrase of Psalm VIII has all the high-sounding weakness of 'State-poetry':

> Il n'est faiblesse égale à nos infirmités;
> Nos plus sages discours ne sont que vanités,
> Et nos sens corrompus n'ont goût qu'à des ordures;
>   Toutefois, ô bon Dieu,
> Nous te sommes si chers, qu'entre tes créatures,
> Si l'ange est le premier, l'homme a le second lieu.[1]

One has a vision of a surpliced God leaning down to reply in an audible whisper: 'Mais parfaitement, Monsieur de Malherbe. Mais l'ordure, c'est un mot un peu barbare, n'est-ce-pas?' It is the only one which unites Malherbe with the world of Donne, whose poetry he would certainly have dismissed, as he did Ronsard's, as uncouth and primitive. He would have had more sympathy, perhaps, with two of his minor successors, who in paraphrasing the 'Song of the Three Children', an apocryphal addition to the Book of Daniel, call loudly and unequivocally on the whole Universe to rejoice in the Lord. The poems of both appear in an anthology of 1660, almost the last in which the Baroque style predominates, and already one of them, Antoine Godeau, was feeling out towards the new strictness of language and versification demanded by Malherbe. Enthusiasm was now frowned on; moderation, even in religious expression, was considered more fitting. The other, however, the Capuchin Martial de Brives, still used all the resources of Baroque extravagance in that verse where the three young men in the fiery furnace call on the seas to bless the hand of the Lord:

---

[1] There is no weakness equal to our imperfections; our wisest words are but vanity, and our corrupt senses have taste only for filth; and yet, o gracious God, we are so dear to you that if the angel is first among your creatures, man is second.

> Vaste océan, monde liquide,
> Lices des carosses ailés
> Que les quatre vents attelés
> Traînent où la fureur les guide,
> Monstre qu'on voit toujours caché
> Et dans votre lit attaché
> Comme un frénétique incurable,
> Baisez d'un flot humilié
> Vos augustes chaînes de sable
> Et bénissez la main qui vous en a lié.[1]

After drawing the sea as a chained madman, in this expansion of one verse of the Bible, the poet passes on to consider the whales of the next verse, 'that are like breathing islands', and the dumb fish, 'inhabitants of hollow, floating palaces built of the marble of the waves'. All is extravagant; all is in movement. Godeau, by contrast, dilating on the same verses, demands formal homage rather than high-sounding praise:

> Mers aux pilotes inconnues,
> Rendez hommage au souverain
> Par qui sur des globes d'airain,
> Vous êtes en haut soutenues:[2]

The last analogy is not based on any image in the 'Song' itself, and does not evoke a clear picture. It is difficult to see why the seas are not sustained on a single globe. By Godeau's day, moreover, there were few seas unknown to pilots. The effect of his poem is attained rather by its speed and its ready evocation than by the habitual Baroque attention to detail. The Baroque style in France was already in decline; after 1660

[1] Vast ocean, liquid world, arena of the winged chariots which the four harnessed winds drag wherever their wild course takes them, monster who always appears to be hidden and fastened to your bed like a raving madman, kiss with humbled waves your noble chains of sand, and bless the hand which tied you to them.

[2] Seas unknown to pilots, give homage to the Sovereign, by whom you are sustained on globes of brass.

most poets opted for classicism, and religious questioning
yielded to psychological curiosity. Racine, for example, in his
'Cantique' based on Romans vii, announces his surprised
discovery that there are two men within him who are often
at odds:

> L'un veut que plein d'amour pour toi
> Mon cœur te soit toujours fidèle.
> L'autre à tes volontés rebelle
> Me révolte contre ta loi.[1]

Such an analysis may lie at the base of a Racinian tragedy.
Its expression is, however, no more poetic than the verses of a
hymn by Isaac Watts. Lyrical poetry was killed in France by
the dictatorship of the scribes, both literary and ecclesiastical,
who limited both its subjects and their treatment. Individual
expression was curtailed, and individuality of style censured
and ridiculed.

The situation in Spain was even less helpful to the poet's
individuality. Here no Malherbe arose; there was no tyranny
of fashion. Nevertheless, the firm suppression of heterodox or
modern ideas, which silenced the social critic Gracián and the
quietest Molinos, had a cramping effect on the poets also.
When writing on religious subjects they were encouraged to
display a simple-minded humility, often very foreign to their
general attitude to the world. Lope de Vega's 'Rimas sacras'
are couched in language so simple as hardly to contain any
original imagery. They are addressed to a Jesus as sentimen-
tally human as a Murillo saint. Completely at variance though
they are with the habitual expression of the phoenix of the
Spanish theatre, one cannot think of the 'Rimas' as unwillingly
written. They are too accomplished for that. Their writing
looks more like an act of voluntary conformity, like that of
many in our modern dictator-states, who are unable to hold
out and make a virtue of their yielding. There is a thin and

---

[1] One wishes that, full of love for you, my heart shall always be faithful
to you. The other, resisting your commands, raises me in rebellion against
you.

polished charm in the dramatist's simple address to the Stranger at the Gates, in which he ruefully reflects on his own hardness of heart:

> ¿Qué tengo yo que mi amistad procuras?
> ¿Qué interés se te sigue, Jesús mío,
> que a mi puerto, cubierto de rocío,
> pasas las noches del invierno oscuras?
> ¡Oh cuánto fueron mis entrañas duras
> pues no te abrí . . .[1]

Lope's questioning is far from urgent. One can perhaps accept the intention of his sonnet as purely decorative, like that of his songs to the Virgin, which adapt the rhythms of folksong 'a lo divino' and deliberately confuse her with a shepherd girl.

> ¿Dónde vais, zagala,
> sola en el monte?[2]

he asks her, and we are reminded that though this was the Virgin, who carried the sun in her womb, other poets had celebrated amorous encounters with other shepherd girls whom they met alone on the mountain. Perhaps the 'Rimas sacras' merely offer a formal submission, in the choicest words the poet could find, to a tyranny of thought too strong for him to resist. Perhaps, however, like lesser men of the time, he rejoiced in his humiliation.

A tougher self-discipline, which causes one voice within him to contend with another, pervades the sonnet 'A Cristo nuestro señor, orando en el huerto' of the Aragonese poet Bartolomé Leonardo de Argensola. His opening question, as he contemplates the Saviour at prayer in the garden, betrays a restlessness that anticipates the despairing faith of Unamuno and Hopkins in our own century:

---

[1] What have I that you sue for my friendship? What interest brings you, dear Jesus, to spend the dark winter nights at my door, covered in dew? Oh, how hard was my heart that I did not open to you!

[2] Where are you going, shepherd-girl, alone on the mountain?

¿Qué estratagema hazéis, guerrero mío?
Mas antes, ¿qué inefable sacramento?
¡Qué os bañe en sangre sólo el pensamiento
de que se llega el plazo al desafío![1]

Argensola then proceeds to reason in theological terms with his Saviour, saying that He cannot wish His sufferings to give Him supernatural strength in order to increase His human courage. At this point the tension of the poem drops, only to increase when the poet finally considers his own sins as the cause of Christ's suffering. The thought of the Crucifixion as a stratagem, and of Christ as a scheming general, has the true Baroque extravagance. Argensola, who was an historian as well as a poet, disapproved strongly both of Góngora's extravagance and Lope's facility. Had he been more single-minded he might have been the Malherbe of Spanish poetry and the Baroque decline might never have occurred. But despite his determined classicism and his military conception of religion, which he expressed also in his Christmas Day sonnet 'Hoy rompe Dios los orbes celestiales' ('Now God forsakes the spheres of heaven'), Argensola shared the fundamental anxiety of his age. Unlike Lope, who offered himself easy comfort in his 'Rimas sacras', Argensola felt himself to be excluded from divine grace. The last lines of his sonnet on the Resurrection express a desolation like that of Milton at the opening of the sonnet on his blindness. Argensola could not make the stoical acceptance which belonged to the character that he endeavoured to assume. Behind the military breastplate was a heart that seemed to call in vain:

o eterno Amor, si al nuevo impulso tuyo
naturaleza en todo el gran distrito
risueña y fuerte aviva el movimento,
¿ por qué yo no lo busco o no lo admito?

[1] What stratagem are you preparing, o my warrior? Or rather what ineffable sacrament? That the mere thought that the time for the struggle is drawing near should bathe you in blood!

¿Yo sólo estéril al fecundo aliento
de la común resurrección me excluyo?[1]

The true Baroque extravagance is also present in a handful
of sonnets by the Mexican friar Miguel de Guevara, whose
most famous poem, 'No me mueve, mi Díos', is generally
printed as anonymous. In it he reasons with God in the
manner of the middle section of Argensola's sonnet on Christ
praying in the Garden, stating the reasons why he would love
Him, even if he did not hope for what he does: a reward in
heaven. In another sonnet, however, which has received far
less notice, Guevara portrays, with a Mexican directness that
was to be imitated later in the century by Luis de Sandoval y
Zapata and Juana de la Cruz, the conflict within him, which
caused him to be at the same time unified and divided, living
and dead, sad and gay:

> Levántame, Señor, que estoy caído,
> sin amor, sin temor, sin fe, sin miedo;
> quiérome levantar, y estoyme quedo;
> yo propio lo deseo y lo impido.
>
> Estoy, siendo uno solo, dividido;
> a un tiempo muero y vivo, triste y ledo;
> lo que puedo hacer, eso no puedo;
> huyo del mal y estoy en él metido.
>
> Tan obstinado estoy en mi porfía,
> que el temor de perderme y de perderte
> jamás de mi mal uso me desvía.
>
> Tu poder y bondad truequen mi suerte:
> que en otros veo enmienda cada día,
> y en mí nuevos deseos de ofenderte.[2]

[1] O eternal love, if Nature smiles on your new impulse throughout a
whole wide region, and strongly quickens her movements, why do I not seek
it and admit it? Why do I alone, in my sterility, shut myself off from the
nourishing breath of the general resurrection?

[2] Raise me, o Lord, for I have fallen, without love, fear, faith or
apprehension. I wish to raise myself and I am supine; I myself desire it and
I prevent it. Though I am one, I am divided; at the same time I am dying
and living, sad and gay. What I am capable of doing that I cannot do, I flee

The sonnet of contradictions was not new in Spanish poetry, nor was the reproachful content of the poem, or the poet's surprise that God could not do more to help him save himself. Argensola described his own similar inability to accept such aid as was proferred to him in his sonnet which begins:

> ¿En qué veré que tu a mi llanto agora,
> Padre benigno, aplicas los oídos . . . ?[1]

Yet from these direct acknowledgements of disunion to Donne's more agonized recognition of his own interior battle there is one vital step. Timid and unhappy bewilderment must give way to a fundamental and uninhibited self-examination. No question must be barred, not even that of belief or disbelief. In Donne's 'Divine Sonnets' the drama is more intense. It is not 'Why cannot you raise me, Lord, for I have fallen', but

> Batter my heart, three person'd God; for, you
> As yet but knocke . . .

There is no mere objective acknowledgement, like Argensola's at the conclusion of his sonnet on Christ in the Garden, that his sin angers the Lord and increases his pain:

> sino como se os viene ante los ojos
> mi culpa, ardéis de generosa ira,
> y en esta lucha aumento vuestras penas.[2]

Donne identifies himself with the suffering Christ. The struggle, as potentially also the Kingdom of Heaven, is within

---

from evil and am engaged in it. I am so obstinate in my perversity, that fear of destroying myself and losing you never deflects me from my wickedness. Your power and goodness reverse my fate. For in others I see betterment every day, and in myself new desires to offend you.

[1] What will show me, kind Father, that you are now listening to my tears . . . ?

[2] But as my guilt comes before your eyes you burn with noble anger, and in this struggle I increase your pains.

him, John Donne. The Crucifixion takes place on the Golgotha of his own soul:

> What if this present were the worlds last night?
> Marke in my heart, O Soule, where thou dost dwell,
> The picture of Christ crucified, and tell
> Whether that countenance can thee afright.

If Bartolomé de Argensola, priest, historian, and conservative critic, revealed some fundamental unease in his religious sonnets, this was not his intention. Guevara, the Mexican friar, was bound to reticence by the rule of his order. Donne, on the other hand, presented himself entire, in the manner of Michelangelo or Shakespeare. He spoke of his physical and spiritual love, drew on all the resources of his scientific learning, freely exposed his fascinated fear of death, and his tortured wish, after the loss of his beloved wife, to devote himself entirely to religion. As poet, lover, and searcher after divinity he was totally committed; and he tells us very plainly indeed how the main strands of his thought and emotion combined, so that love of woman led to love of God:

> Since she whom I lov'd hath payd her last debt
> To Nature, and to hers, and my good is dead,
> And her Soule early into heaven ravished,
> Wholly on heavenly things my mind is sett.
> Here the admyring her my mind did whett
> To seek thee God . . .

Not only does Donne clearly expound the relationship between these two levels of love. He also tells of another duality which could not be reconciled—that between the two Churches, Protestant and Catholic. Donne did not find it as easy to choose as Marino, for whom the matter was one of black or white. His sonnet on Luther is no more than a catalogue of abuse:

> Volpe malvagia, che'l terren fiorito
> ' de la vigna di Cristo incavi e rodi;

> lupo fellon, che con furtive frodi
> il fido ovile hai lacero e tradito . . .[1]

The Huguenot poet Sponde, with many of his fellow-Frenchmen, made a political submission to Rome in the interests of common sense and national prosperity, and ceased to be a poet. Like his king, he knew that this compromise was the sole way of ending the rancour of the Civil War. Otherwise France would have been like Spain, both in the seventeenth century and today: a country in which old feuds are never forgotten. Donne, on the other hand, though advancing in the Church of England to the office of Dean of St Paul's, still asks which is the true Spouse of Christ:

> is it She, which on the other shore
> Goes richly painted? or which rob'd and tore
> Laments and mourns in Germany and here?
> Sleeps she a thousand, then peepes up one yeare?
> Is she selfe truth and errs? now new, now outwore?

His only certainty lies in his passion. Reasoning this way and that, he widens the field of radiation of his poetry, yet at the same time directs the whole of its heat to one spot: his own heart which is so ill-prepared to face an ever-impending death and judgement, yet which trusts, unlike Argensola's, in an ultimate grace:

> Oh my blacke Soule! now thou art summoned
> By sicknesse, deaths herald, and champion;
> Thou art like a pilgrim, which abroad hath done
> Treason, and durst not turne to whence hee is fled,
>   Or like a thiefe, which till deaths doome be read,
> Wisheth himselfe delivered from prison;
> But damn'd and hal'd to execution,
> Wisheth that still he might be imprisoned.
>   Yet grace, if thou repent, thou canst not lacke . . .

---

[1] Villainous fox who hollowed and gnawed the flowery plot of Christ's vine; wicked wolf who with his furtive deceits has torn and betrayed the faithful flock.

Beside Donne's agonized but sure-footed reasoning, expressed in the simple imagery of treason, prison, and execution, an experience common among Elizabethan gentlemen, La Ceppède's prayer to the Saviour to descend into the hell of his soul and save him stumbles among hyperboles and conceits:

> Fais, mon Sauveur, descente en l'Enfer de mon âme:
> Mon âme est un Enfer tout noir d'aveuglement,
> Que l'acéré tranchant de cent remords entame,
> Que sept traîtres Démons traitent journellement,
>   D'un seul point, mon Enfer le nom d'enfer dément
> (Dissemblable à l'Enfer de l'éternelle flamme)
> C'est qu'on n'espère plus en l'éternel tourment:
> Et dans le mien j'espère, et ta grace réclame.[1]

La Ceppède's poem is carried forward on a tide of rhetoric. No individual image makes a clear impact. In fact the rapid shift from the blackness of the second line to the sharp sword of the third, and thence to the seven devils who feed the poet's remorse, is visually bewildering. Donne's move, by contrast, from the 'pilgrim which abroad hath done treason' to the thief awaiting sentence and then receiving his doom, heightens the tension and strengthens the analogy between the poet's state and the prison in which both captives languish. The images are of the simplest, yet they are marked with Donne's personal imprint.

Andreas Gryphius, on the other hand, crying to the Holy Ghost to save him from a similar state of dereliction, looks for no original imagery but resorts to a simple series of invocations of mounting intensity, united only by the theme of contrast between the poet's present condition and that for which he prays:

[1] Descend, my Saviour, into the hell of my soul: my soul is a black hell of blindness, cut by the sharp blades of endless remorse, which seven treacherous Devils feed every day. In one respect, my hell disclaims the name of hell (unlike the Hell of eternal fire): in eternal torment one has no more hope, but in mine I hope and call on your grace.

Ich irre, führe mich, Verstand, auf rechte Wege!
Ich zweifle, Wahrheit! Steh mit deiner Weisheit bei!
Ich diene, Freiheit! Reisz die harten Band entzwei!
    Ich zittre, Schutz! Halt auf des Himmels Donnerschläge!
Ich schwind, o Ewigkeit! Erhalte für und für!
O Leben aller Ding! Ich sterbe, leb in mir![1]

Like much of Gryphius' work, this sonnet goes beyond
the bounds of individual statement into a middle kingdom,
like that inhabited by St John of the Cross, halfway between
poetry and religious meditation. For every line contains echoes
of familiar statements. Only the organization bears the poet's
individual stamp, though even here without his signature its
authorship might be attributed to any one of the numerous
compatriots who suffered from the same existential anxiety.
Gryphius' use of paradox and contradiction, which sometimes descends into chop-logic, was not his own. La Ceppède
used it freely, as can be seen in his prayer to the Saviour,
quoted above; and Donne raised it to a far higher and more
individual pitch in 'Good Friday, 1613. Riding Westward'.

Here the argument, which is based on the similarities and
contradictions between the actual sunset of that day and the
sunrise of Christ's sacrifice on the Cross, which was also a
setting, might seem essentially unpoetic. Indeed it belongs in
the category of schoolmen's reasoning, a monkish pastime for
which the taste was declining in the seventeenth century. Yet
Donne brilliantly revives it, and uses it to illustrate the
common distraction in which he, like all other men, passes his
life:

Pleasure or businesse, so, in our Soules admit
For their first mover, and are whirld by it,
Hence is't, that I am carryed towards the West
This day, when my Soules forme bends towards the East.

[1] I am astray, Lead me, Reason, on the right path! I am in doubt,
Truth! Stand by me with your wisdom! I am in slavery, Freedom! Rend my
hard bonds asunder! I tremble, Protector! Ward off the heavens' thunder-
bolts! I faint, Eternity! Support me utterly! O life-principle of all things! I
am dying. Live in me!

> There I should see a Sunne, by rising set,
> And by that setting endless day beget;
> But that Christ on this Crosse, did rise and fall,
> Sinne had eternally benighted all.

The word-play of rising and setting may appear in itself
trivial. Yet it leads by way of the symbol of the Cross, a form
which contains and reconciles all opposites, to the thought of
sin and night, which would have been man's eternal lot if the
sun had not risen on the first Good Friday. The argumentative
conceits have fulfilled the purpose of throwing the statement
which follows them into higher emotional relief. La Ceppède's
five repetitions of 'Enfer', on the other hand, serve only to
weaken his very correct theological statement, that in his hell
he has hope and invokes God's grace.

The power of Donne's last poems lies in their treatment of
some extremely complicated and seemingly prosaic propositions. In his 'Hymne to God my God, in my sicknesse',
written, according to Walton, eight days before he died, he
uses the double meaning of the Latin word *fretum* (raging heat
and strait) and the fact that on a flat map, which has not yet
been pasted on a globe—and which represents the poet lying
flat on his bed—the extreme points will be the same to
reconcile the paradox that through the strait of death he will
reach eternal life, and that death and resurrection are one:

> Whilst my Physitians by their love are growne
>   Cosmographers, and I their mapp, who lie
> Flat on this bed, that by them may be showne
>   That this is my South-west discoverie
>   *Per fretum febris*, by these streights to die.
> I joy, that in these straits I see my West;
>   For, though theire currants yeeld return to none,
> What shall my West hurt me? As West and East
>   In all flatt Maps (and I am one) are one,
>   So death doth touch the Resurrection.

La Ceppède treats the Resurrection as an external event.
Devout Christian though he was, he had related Christ's

sojourn on earth to the descent of Prometheus who brought fire to his creation Man, and in speaking of the Crucifixion had compared Christ to the phoenix. Now, in speaking of the Resurrection, he mingled conventionally poetic with quaint and commonplace language. On the one hand, the Saviour's body is more precious than all the gold of the gold-bearing river Pactolus; on the other, it is drawn from the tomb, into which it has been well corked ('bouché'), by the rays of the guiding sun. Christ thus becomes, in alchemical terms, a solar figure. Yet when La Ceppède actually defines the mystery of the Resurrection his analogies are rather flat:

> Ce mystère est partout marqué par la nature:
> La lumière se meurt à l'abord de la nuit,
> Puis revit, et reluit: le grain sous la culture
> De la terre se meurt, puis nombreux se produit.
> Nous voyons tous les jours des arbres choir leur
> fruit . . .[1]

La Ceppède is at times strangely uneven. The angel at the tomb, so he tells us, appears to the Marys in a white body because white is the colour of the victorious Christ and the earnest of the angels' future glory. Yet when he assures the ladies ('Les Dames') that the Resurrection has taken place it is in formal language which foreshadows that of some minor Racinian character:

> Il est ressuscité; partez, volez légères,
> Soyez de cet advis les promptes messagers
> Aux siens, même à Pierre, élu chef du troupeau.[2]

La Ceppède relates the story in his usual slow-motion, but conveys no sense of having been an eye-witness, and still less

[1] This mystery is everywhere observed in Nature. Light dies at the coming of night, then revives and shines again. The seed dies at the ploughing of the earth and then multiplies. Every day we see the trees drop their fruit . . .

[2] He is brought back to life; fly swiftly and be the speedy messengers of this news to his followers, even to Peter, the chosen head of the band.

that the death and resurrection of Christ were in some sort his own, as they were Donne's.

George Herbert has much in common with La Ceppède. Like him he makes play with typology: Old Testament characters and events are chosen to represent those of the New. In 'Peace' the poet seeking for rest meets Melchizedek, of whom he says:

> There was a Prince of old
> At Salem dwelt, where liv'd with good increase
>   Of flock and fold.
> He sweetly liv'd; yet sweetness did not save
>   His life from foes.
> But after death out of his grave
> There sprang twelve stalks of wheat:
> Which many wondring at, got some of those
>   To plant and set.

For the 'King of Salem, which is, King of Peace' (Heb. vii, 2) prefigured Christ; and his act in giving wine and bread to Abraham is the Old Testament 'type' of Christ's feeding of his Church. Christ is the god who nourishes, the Priest who officiates, the King and the sacrifice.[1]

This is a Holy Communion poem; it is also a poem of the Apostles' mission, and of *Corpus Christi* as the bread and, at the same time, the mystical body of Christ. The doctrine is concise and full of considered ambiguities. But the poem is, at the same time, unlike most of La Ceppède's, a personal statement. Herbert's collection is called *The Temple*. Its subject is the Church, of which men may become 'very members incorporate', and it draws for its imagery on the traditional architecture and ceremonial of the Church, also on mediaeval poetry and the iconography of its stained glass and illuminated missals. But it is concerned even more closely with Herbert, whose heart is a place of worship, and who as a clergyman acts as the representative of Everyman. He is himself the high-priest Aaron, who speaks in the poem of that name:

[1] See Rosemond Tuve, *A Reading of George Herbert*, pp. 161–2.

> Profaneness in my head,
> Defects and darknesse in my breast,
> A noise of passions ringing me for dead
> Unto a place where is no rest:
> In him I am well drest.

In 'The Sacrifice' Herbert speaks as Christ, in the first person, uttering the paradoxes, and pointing an irony that is only evident to a reader who is as permeated with the thought of the Church as Herbert himself:

> Then on my head a crown of thorns I wear;
> For these are all the grapes Zion doth bear,
> Though I my vine planted and watred there
> Was ever grief like mine?

The implied associations are many, but the root meaning is that though he has planted and watered the vine or house of Israel, in himself and in mankind, it bears for grapes only this bitter thorny crown. Herbert's poetry expresses a supreme paradox; it is personal and impersonal at the same time, because when he writes as a poet it is with that part of himself which is immortal man.

At times Herbert expresses the thought and knowledge of a scholar and wit, as learned and resourceful as Donne, only to renounce it. At the beginning, as he says in 'Jordan (II)',

> Thousands of notions in my brain did runne,
> Off'ring their service, if I were not sped:
> I often blotted what I had begunne;
> This was not quick enough, and that was dead.
> Nothing could seem too rich to clothe the sunne,
> Much lesse those joyes which trample on his head . . .

yet in the concluding lines of this poem a friend (who is God) whispers to him:

> How wide is all this long pretence!
> There is in love a sweetnesse ready penn'd:
> Copie out that and save expense.

Later, however, in 'The Forerunners' Herbert stated that it was not really necessary for him to wash himself in the 'Jordan' of simplicity. These learned conceits now seemed to him the best he had, and he resolved to turn them to a holy use:

> Farewell sweet phrases, lovely metaphors.
> But will ye leave me thus? when ye before
> Of stewes and brothels only knew the doores,
> Then did I wash you with my tears, and more,
>   Brought you to Church well drest and clad:
> My God must have my best, ev'n all I had.

Herbert therefore felt free to retain his individuality of expression, and even at times to play with words in the manner of Donne, for

> Beautie and beauteous words should go together.

Yet at the conclusion of this poem, in which he seems to look back on his whole life's achievement in poetry, he proclaims, apostrophizing the language he has used, that

> . . . *Thou art still my God*, is all that ye
> Perhaps with more embellishment can say.

Herbert was not a mystic; of the identity between the spark in him and the fire of divinity, unlike Vaughan and Traherne, he had nothing to say. Nevertheless, like them, he walked with God as a friend. He wrote of God's Church and identified himself with it. He was a vessel of God's will, a window through which His light could pass to others. In himself he knew that he was valueless. Asking how he could preach, he gave the answer that he must illumine the doctrine he stated by his own life, since without that words counted for nothing:

Lord, how can man preach thy eternall word?
  He is a brittle, crazie glasse:
Yet in thy temple thou dost him afford
  This glorious and transcendent place,
  To be a window, through thy grace.
But when thou dost anneal in glasse thy storie,
  Making thy life to shine within
Thy holy preachers; then the light and glorie
  More rev'rend grows, & more doth win:
  Which else shows watrish, bleak & thin.
Doctrine and life, colours and light, in one
  When they combine and mingle, bring
A strong regard and awe but speech alone
  Doth vanish like a flaring thing,
  And in the eare, not conscience ring.

Much of the poetry that was written under the dictatorship of the scribes of the Counter-Reformation rings magnificently in the ear. But the poet and his poetry are not one. The glass is decorative, but the colours are ill-balanced, the black of despair and the red of violence overbalancing the blue of serenity and the green of nature. Herbert rejoices where others despair and seek shelter beneath the pleasure domes of art, or in the green shade of an island refuge. The peace for which Donne strove in his battle between the spirit and the flesh was achieved with less stress, it is true, but with an equally unflinching resolution by his heir and successor, George Herbert.

9

The ring of light

GEORGE HERBERT'S poetry stands on the borderline between the religious and the mystical. For while it speaks of deep personal experience, it invariably does so in the context of church doctrine. The 'Temple' of his title was at the same time the church in which he preached and worshipped, and his own heart in which he contemplated the mysteries of God. Christ was not for him, as He was for Lope, Argensola, Malherbe, and Crashaw, an external figure whose existence lay in a distant historical time, and whose drama was to be interpreted only in terms of ritual and theology. Nor, on the other hand, did Herbert adopt the extreme standpoint of the mystical poets, English and German, for whom Christ was primarily a personal experience, and who felt themselves to have been born and to move in the Eternity of the New Testament. The mystics spoke always from their highest experience, without bitterly relating it, as Donne and Herbert did, to the contrasting and lower levels of experience in which they habitually lived. For the mystics there was no darkness, only a light that was sometimes veiled. Herbert, on the other hand, saw his light the more clearly because of the contrasting gloom outside his church.

In the poem 'Aaron' Herbert places the two extreme poles of existence in close juxtaposition. First we are shown a state of distraction which a more theologically minded poet might have personified as the devil; then we are told of its opposite; and each state is defined in terms of a particular music. For Herbert was an auditory not a visual poet, and his love of music is evident both in the singing quality of his lines and from Walton's remark that 'the greatest diversion from his study was the practice of music, of which he became a great master'.[1]

Both the noise of his distraction and another music that was capable of calming him are succinctly described:

> Profanenesse in my head,
> Defects and darknesse in my breast,
> A noise of passions ringing me for dead
> Unto a place where is no rest.
> Poore priest thus am I drest.
> Only another head
> I have, another heart and breast,
> Another musick, making live not dead,
> Without whom I could have no rest:
> In him I am well drest.

In the poem's last verses Herbert discovers that this second state is Christ:

> Christ is my onely head,
> My alone onely heart and breast,
> Another musick, striking me ev'n dead;
> That to the old man I may rest,
> And be in him new drest.

Herbert's 'Temple' represented only secondarily the building of stone and glass. Primarily it was, to use the words of a sermon by his contemporary Lancelot Andrewes, formed of his own flesh and bone.

> So come we to have two sorts of Temples [wrote Andrewes]; Temples of flesh and bone, as well as Temples of lime and stone. For if our bodies be termed houses, because our souls, tenant-wise, abide and dwell in them; if because our souls dwell they be houses, if God do so they be temples: why not? why not?[2]

---

[1] *Lives of Donne, Walton*, etc. (World's Classics), p. 269.
[2] Quoted by Joseph H. Summers, *George Herbert*, p. 85.

Central to Herbert's imagery, notes Summers,[1] is the creator and architect who formed these two sorts of temple, and also the symbolical third, which was the institutional church and which united the other two.

Herbert's poetry is constructed with the same architectural complexity as the 'Temple'—upon three levels—which is its subject. His mastery of consonance and dissonance, indeed, is as great as that of any English poet. In the poem 'Aaron', already quoted, for example, he repeats the identical rhyme-words five times, the number of stanzas corresponding to the numbers of letters in the high-priest's name. Between the first two stanzas quoted, moreover, as between all the rest, there is a strong contrast of mood; the first is cacophonous with a break at the end of each line, and a jangle of p's, d's, and b's, while the second runs more smoothly without discordant vowels. In this way natural man is contrasted with the true or inner self, whose heart is the temple of the true God. The pattern of sound is not finally resolved, however, until the final stanza. Herbert wrote some of his poems in a hieroglyph, or even shaped them, like the Greek poets of Alexandria, to represent their subject pictorially on the printed page. Thus 'Easter Wings' has the form of two butterflies, the length of line diminishing towards the middle of each stanza, which represents the creature's body, and expanding again towards the wing-tips at the end. One is reminded of the nine canons of increasing complication in Bach's 'Musical Offering' which, while solving technical problems which had engaged the unsuccessful attentions of all his Baroque predecessors, are at the same time consummate works of art. Indeed they must have pleased the amateur flautist Frederick the Great, who set Bach his theme, as much as the musical theorists in their organ-lofts who tried out his triumphant solutions. The greater the feats of composition which this master musician set himself, the higher his inspiration mounted. Similarly, though in a minor degree, Herbert was able to turn an anagram on the name 'Jesu' into a shapely though minor poem.

Whereas Herbert appears to have conceived his poems as a

[1] Op. cit., p. 89.

whole, each stanza contributing towards a final effect or resolution, and 'The Temple' itself forming a complete hieroglyph of a man in the inner and outer sanctuaries of 'flesh and bone' and 'lime and stone', Henry Vaughan, though he proclaimed himself Herbert's disciple, and sometimes based his poems on models taken from 'The Temple', is far less perfect in his detail and far less musical than his master. Reaching out above even the most sublime architecture towards the primal light, he would begin a poem from an insight into Biblical truth or a moment of vision, which may be seen to diminish in intensity as the poem develops. The conclusion of a poem by Vaughan is seldom as strong and compelling as its opening. The light which informs its first stanzas has faded, as a moment of mystical illumination loses its intensity when the discovery that has been vouchsafed is translated into words and images.

Vaughan was, from the first, not much moved by the stock Baroque themes. In his preface to his sacred poems, which he published in 1650 under the title *Silex Scintillans* ('The Sparkling Flint'), he declared his independence of the Metaphysicals: 'Those ingenious persons, which in the late notions are termed *wits*.' What he particularly objected to was the importation of '*Foreign vanities*; so that the most lascivious compositions of *France* and *Italy* are here naturalized and made *English*'. At the same time he invoked 'the blessed man, Mr George Herbert, whose holy *life* and *verse* gained many pious *Converts* (of whom I am the least)'. In imitation of Herbert, he 'begged leave to communicate this my poor *talent* to the *Church*'.

Vaughan differs from his master in that, despite this declaration, his poetry is not dedicated to the Church but celebrates a personal vision expressed in terms of ideas that, basically, were not Christian but Gnostic or Neo-platonic. These ideas had a particular appeal to Vaughan on account of his medical training, since they suggested a congruence between the body, soul, and spirit of man, and a greater trinity which could be thought of as the body, soul, and spirit of the Universe. The dominant conception in this cosmology, which was at the same time spiritual and scientific, was the doctrine that man is the microcosm of the Universe.

These beliefs confirmed a cardinal intuition in Vaughan's early life, an apprehension of the unity between himself, the world of Nature, and the heavenly sphere. All his best poems arise from a transcendent certainty, founded on this experience, that all is right in the Universe. The chief preoccupation in his poetry was with the fluctuations of this awareness; with the descent from those rare moments of illumination, which had been continuous in his childhood, to the dead level of his less inspired living. The unevenness of his poetry, in fact, reflects the repeated veilings throughout his life of the visionary light which shines out from his finest lines. He states this case clearly in the opening of the poem 'Repentance':

> Lord, since thou didst in this vile Clay
>   That sacred Ray
> Thy spirit plant, quickning the whole
> With that one grains Infused wealth,
> My forward flesh creept on, and subtly stole
> Both growth, and power; Checking the health
> And heat of thine: That little gate
> And narrow way, by which to thee
> The Passage is, He term'd a grate
> And Entrance to Captivatie.

Full though it is of echoes from Herbert's 'H.Baptism (II)', this poem enshrines the core of Vaughan's faith. Without any hard and fast doctrine of pre-existence, he believes, on the evidence of his own greater awareness in childhood, that each adult man, repeating the history of Adam, has been expelled from the state of Paradise, that as the 'forward flesh creept on', so the grain or essence implanted in his clay has been stifled in its growth. Now the narrow way that leads back to God seems only a prison-gate, and

> Thy Promises but empty words
> Which none but Children heard, or taught.

Against this arid state Vaughan pits his memory of such moments of insight as that recorded in the opening of 'The World'—'I saw Eternity the other night'. This experience had a double character; not only did it bring the poet into relation with the divine order above him but also with the world of Nature below him, which retained its purity since it did not partake of the Fall.

So, foreshadowing the pantheistic poets of the nineteenth century, Vaughan turned for comfort in his state of sin or separation to

> The blades of grasse, thy Creatures feeding,
> The trees, their leafs; the flowers, their seeding;
> The Dust, of which I am a part,
> The Stones much softer than my heart,
> The drops of rain, the sighs of wind,
> The Stars to which I am stark blind,
> The Dew thy herbs drink up by night,
> The beams they warm them at i' th'light,
> All that have signature or life.

Nature is now an earnest to the poet of this deeper communion from which he is cut off by sin. His sense of sin, however, is free from self-reproach; he merely acknowledges that now he is 'stark-blind' to the stars. The significance of the stars is determined by Vaughan's belief in astrology. Blindness to them implies not a failure to observe the heavenly motions but a forgetfulness of the laws governing his own destiny. To move in harmony with the movements of the stars, or with the laws of his own fate, brings happiness. But man is not generally awake to this possibility, which he has known in childhood. He does not 'watch'. In 'The Constellation' Vaughan sees on one side 'Silence, and light, and watchfulness', and on the other 'poor man', who

> Still either sleeps, or slips his span.

But there may be times when he will wake, and it would be better for him to sleep:

Perhaps some nights hee'l watch with you, and peep
    When it were best to sleep,
Dares know Effects, and Judge them long before,
    When th'herb he treads knows much, much more.

Vaughan seems here, in a later verse of 'The Constellation', to
be warning against a philosophical judgement in advance of
experience or understanding. For he believed that there was a
greater wisdom in Nature than in man, though this wisdom
existed in the child before he began to exercise self-will and
set himself up in opposition to that destiny which is written in
the stars. It is clear that Vaughan retained a preternaturally
clear memory of that childish state, and from the evidence of
the opening lines of 'The World' it can be taken that this
memory was refreshed by occasional returns of his illumination. But how to recover permanently this condition of higher
perception and obedience is a question to which he can find no
certain answer. The need, as he sees it in the 'The Retreate',
is to travel not forwards but back:

> O how I long to travell back
> And tread again that ancient track!
> That I might once more reach that plaine,
> Where first I left my glorious traine,
> From whence th'Inlightned spirit sees
> That shady City of Palme trees. . . .

The poet's longing is to regain this early enlightenment in
order that he may

> In that state I came return.

But the words 'back' and 'backward' had for him a more
profound significance than that of a mere return. The
direction they implied was, in some sense, at right angles to
the flow of time. At the height of his vision he had glimpsed a
direction that was neither backwards nor forwards; he had
seen Eternity in the figure of a ring. The metaphor occurs

three times in his poetry. At its first appearance, in the poem
'To Amoret, Walking in a Starry Evening', the ring seems to be
a symbol of the Universe. But when it recurs in 'The World':

> I saw Eternity the other night
> Like a great Ring of pure and endless light,
>   All calm as it was bright . . .

this ring of Eternity appears to lie above the centre of life, since

> . . . round beneath it, Time in hours, days, years,
>   Driv'n by the spheres
> Like a vast shadow mov'd . . .

So time is illusory, no more than a shadow in the light of
Eternity. Vaughan probably drew these images from Plato's
'Timaeus' and the Gnostic Hermetica.

In its third appearance in 'Vanity of Spirit' this ring takes
the form of a circle which encloses the world of corruption.
Eternity, therefore, is both a boundary, being more apparent
at the moments of birth and death, and also an element in the
midst of which we exist, to be attained not by a journey
forwards or backwards, but by a reaching up in the midst of
life. This reaching up required no effort in childhood, and will
require none again if, before death, the simplicity of childhood
can be recaptured. Often Vaughan refers to Paradise as a place
to which he can go while still alive. In 'The Night' he pleads:

> Were all my loud, evil days
> Calm and unhaunted as is thy dark Tent,
> Whose peace but by some Angels wing òr voice
>   Is seldom rent;
> Then I in Heaven all the long year
> Would keep, and never wander here.

Death, one may conclude, and awakening, and the return
to a vision of Eternity, comprised a single 'backward' idea for
Vaughan; they were a possibility not only beyond the grave

but in the midst of life. In this statement he was not specific, being no philosopher but a poet. But what separated him from this desired state he clearly defined in the conclusion of 'Cockcrowing':

> Onely this Veyle which thou hast broke,
> And must be broken yet in me,
> This veyle, I say, is all the cloke
> And cloud which shadows thee from me.
>> This veyle thy full-ey'd love denies,
>> And only gleams and fractions spies.

Vaughan's is a poetry of 'gleams and fractions', and thus corresponds to the fluctuating nature of his illumination. The surface of his poems shines with no constant light, yet like his flint throws off repeated and splendid sparks, which are sometimes brighter than those of his masters, Donne and Herbert.

Thomas Traherne was a less skilful poet than Vaughan. His finest passages, indeed, are to be found in his prose *Centuries of Meditation*. He began, however, from the same childish experience of the unity of self and nature. In his eyes all origins were pure, all developments liable to a corruption from which they could only be rescued by 'Thought', a process which he seems to have identified with religious contemplation; a function which he held to be absent in the perceptive child, but capable in adult life of calling the lost experiences of childhood back into existence. This he clearly states in the poem 'Thoughts (I)':

> The Ey's confind, the Body pent
> In narrow Room: Lims are of small Extent.
>> But Thoughts are always free.
>> And as they're best,
> So can they even in the Brest,
>> Rove ore the World with Libertie:
>> Can enter Ages, Present be
> In Any Kingdom, into Bosoms see
>> Thoughts, Thoughts can come to Things, and view,
> What Bodies cant approach unto.

But in the beginning apprehensions had been immediate. The 'shades of the prison-house', which were in a later century to close round the growing Wordsworth, were represented for Traherne by the walls of his prosperous uncle's inn at Hereford where he came to live on the death or disappearance of his indigent parents. Here, among the bustle of arriving and departing guests, which he indirectly refers to both in his verse and prose, he first met 'Solitude'. He found it also in these lanes and fields where once he had been conscious of unseen presences. He describes his loss of that childish sense of the supernatural in the poem 'Solitude', which survives only in a version prepared for a publication which did not take place, and probably altered by his brother Philip:

> Remov'd from Town,
> From People, Churches, Feasts, and Holidays,
> The Sword of State, the Mayor's Gown,
> And all the Neighb'ring Boys;
> As if no Kings
> On Earth there were, or living Things,
> The silent Skies salute mine Eys, the Seas
> My Soul surround; no Rest I found, or Eas.
> My roving Mind
> Search'd every Corner of the spacious Earth,
> From Sky to Sky, if it could find,
> (But found not) any Mirth:
> Not all the Coasts,
> Nor all the great and glorious Hosts,
> In Hev'n or Earth, did any Mirth afford;
> I pin'd for hunger at a plenteous Board.

Traherne's sense of reality was far stronger than Vaughan's. Despite the wilful primitiveness of his language, and the curious repetition of words and phrases—'Earth' occurs three times in the two stanzas quoted—it would be wrong to regard the poet of this 'Solitude', which differs so entirely from the melancholy poem on the same subject by Saint-Amant and from Góngora's consummately contrived 'Soledades', as a primitive. Traherne was a scholar and a Platonist, who spent much of his life in Oxford. He was also a specialist in early Church history. If he described a view that embraced both horizons as one 'from Sky to Sky', and in another wrote tautologously of 'a Small and little thing', it was because he wished to match childish vision with the language of childhood. For he was conscious of his inability to record his early emotional experiences with their original directness. Once the seer and the seen had been one. Now it was left to the adult scholar, with the aid of the 'thought' which the child had not required, to reconstruct and relive the past. Thus childish memories could be made to nourish maturity, and mature thought to enrich the remembered moments of deeper awareness. The poem 'Shadows in the Water', with its several layers of symbolism, demonstrates the poet's reliance on this 'circulation' or two-way traffic between the present and the past. For he could express nothing without first 'borrowing Matter' (his own phrase) from his memory. The poem may have owed its conception to a passage in Plotinus. But its borrowed matter, without which it could not have been expressed, was a moment of childhood, in which the poet, while playing with some other children beside a still pond, had been fascinated by the reflection of himself and his friends in the water. 'Shadows in the Water', of which we have only Philip Traherne's no doubt somewhat conventionalized version, is tied to the world of objects and bodies by its concrete imagery. We see the children by the pond-side just as in 'Solitude' we saw the mayoral procession pass through long-ago Hereford, with Traherne's uncle the mayor at its head. When Traherne comes to describe the celestial city the pitch of its roofs likewise suggests this border city in which he passed his childhood.

In 'Shadows in the Water', a childish manner of reasoning is made to serve the purpose of profound metaphysical statement. The vision of his looking-glass country is as circumstantial as Alice's:

Beneath the Water People drown'd.
Yet with another Hev'n crown'd,
In spacious Regions seem'd to go
Freely moving to and fro:
    In bright and open Space
    I saw their very face;
Eys, Hands, and Feet they had like mine;
Another Sun did with them shine.
'Twas strange that People there should walk,
And yet I could not hear them talk:
That throu a little watry Chink,
Which one dry Ox or Horse might drink,
    We other Worlds should see,
    Yet not admitted be;
And other Confines there behold
Of light and Darkness, Heat and Cold.
I call'd them oft, but call'd in vain;
No Speeches we could entertain:
Yet did I there expect to find
Som other World, to pleas my Mind.
    I plainly saw by these
    A new Antipodes,
Whom, tho they were so plainly seen,
A Film kept off that stood between.

Though cut off from this other world by the water's surface and
his body's 'narrow room', the poet yet sees in his vision of it the
certain promise that

    Som unknown Joys there be
    Laid up in Store for me;
  To which I shall, when that thin Skin
  Is broken, be admitted in.

Compared with Traherne, Vaughan seems to have felt no
great love for Nature. His gleams and flashes light up the
landscape of his mind, but give his reader no sight of the Welsh
hills among which he passed his days. His poems are set in a
Bible country such as he must have imagined it in his youth.

It has few recognizable details; water-falls, streams and palm-trees, though mentioned, have no outline or individuality, nor do they belong together in a single country.

The landscape of the German poets, who shared the religious certainty if not the mystical experience of Vaughan and Traherne, is equally generalized. One cannot localize the woodlands, cattle, men, or cities on which Paul Gerhardt sees the sun setting in the first verse of his 'Abendlied' ('evening-song') in any definite land:

> Nun ruhen alle Wälder,
> Vieh, Menschen, Städt und Felder,
> Es schläft die ganze Welt:
> Ihr aber, meine Sinnen,
> Auf, auf, ihr sollt beginnen
> Was eurem Schöpfer wohlgefällt.[1]

The sun sets, the light disappears, the golden stars glitter in the deep blue hall of heaven, and all is ready for the body to rest in the care of Jesus and the angelic host. Gerhardt's language is as childlike as Traherne's but rather less individual and more naïve. In one verse the poet compares himself to a chicken, protected from Satan's jaws by the broad wings of the Redeemer. Gerhardt, a Lutheran pastor, wrote his poems to the measures of hymn-tunes, and many of them still keep their places in the hymn books. He was, moreover, the poet on whom Bach drew most freely for the texts of his cantatas: no less than sixteen make use of Gerhardt's verses. The meditation 'An das leidende Angesicht Jesu Christi' ('On the suffering countenance of Christ')—from which Bach's Passion chorale 'O Haupt voll Blut und Wunden' is taken—is somewhat affected by the prevailing addiction to charnel-house detail, from which Gerhardt was, on the whole, freer than his contemporaries. Yet when, in this poem, he contemplates the Saviour, he sees His face pale with approaching death and red

---

[1] Now all the woods are at rest, cattle, men, town and country, the whole world is asleep. But, you, my senses, arise, arise, you must begin the work that pleases your Creator.

with the blood that flows from His thorn-crowned brow. Gerhardt's best poetry, however, is an expression of simple rejoicing. At the opening of his 'Sommergesang', he tells his heart to go out and seek pleasure in the summer gardens that bloom for him. His catalogue of their beauties is conventional. He uses no metaphysical imagery, and his descriptions are not always free from preciosity. Yet the poem has no difficulty in arousing a mood of simple happiness:

> Die Bäume stehen voller Laub,
> Das Erdreich decket seinen Staub
> Mit einem grünen Kleide.
> Narcissus und die Tulipan
> Die ziehen sich viel schöner an,
> Als Salomonis Seide.
> Die Lerche schwingt sich in die Luft,
> Das Täublein fleugt aus seiner Kluft
> Und macht sich in die Wälder;
> Der hochbegabte Nachtigall
> Ergötzt und füllt mit ihrem Schall
> Berg, Hügel, Tal und Felder.[1]

Compared with Marvell surveying the gardens of Appleton House, Gerhardt makes very little of his tulip-beds and his narcissi. Nor does he allow his 'highly gifted nightingale' to do more than fill the valleys with her voice. Variations on her song in the manner of Marino and Crashaw were far from Gerhardt's purpose, which was to strike a proper balance between personal expression and the needs of a simple and pious audience or congregation. No poem by George Herbert, though he was as good a churchman as the German, would lend itself to be set or sung. Nor would the more individual poetry of the best of Gerhardt's Catholic contemporaries, Friedrich von Spee, seem so suitable for the text of a chorale. His poem on the ox and the ass beside the manger ('Vom

[1] The trees stand thick with foliage, the earth covers her dust with a green dress. Narcissus and Tulip dress themselves in finer cloth than Solomon's silk. The lark soars into the air, the dove flies out of its cleft and makes off into the woods. The highly gifted nightingale delights the mountains, hills, valleys and fields, filling them with her noise.

Ochs und Eselein bei der Krippen') begins like the echo of a
folksong:

> Der Wind auf leeren Straszen
> Streckt aus die Flügel sein,
> Streicht hin gar scharf ohn Maszen
> Zur Bethlems Krippen ein;
> Er brummelt hin und wieder,
> Der fliegend Winterbot,
> Greift an die Gleich und Glieder
> Dem frisch vermenschten Gott.[1]

Spee, a Jesuit whose unhappy duty it was to take the
confessions of some two hundred convicted witches in the
diocese of Würzburg, was a more agitated and more ecstatic
poet than Gerhardt. His Würzburg experience turned him
into a fervent opponent of sorcery trials; and his delight in the
beauty of the world, which was as strong as Traherne's, threw
him back on his own sorrow and loneliness. Spee ecstatically
calls on the whole Universe to praise the Lord. But as he
invokes the dragon in his hole, the whale in the deep, smoke
and fire and the dread lightning, we see that he has altogether
ceased to look at Nature. His mind's eye has opened and his
physical eye has closed:

> Auch lobet Gott von Erden auf,
> Ihr Drachen aus den Klüften,
> Ihr Walfisch tief aus salzem Sauf,
> Wind, Saus und Braus in Lüften.
> Auch Hagel weisz, auch Flocken greis,
> Von Schnee und Eis entzogen;
> Auch Dämpf und Feur, Blitz ungeheur,
> Zusamt dem Regenbogen.[2]

[1] The wind spreads its wings in the empty streets, and blows with the
utmost keenness into the manger at Bethlehem. It roars hither and thither,
the flying herald of winter, and chills the joints and limbs of this God newly
made man.

[2] Praise God also from the earth, you dragons from your holes, you
whales from deep in the salty drink, wind, riot and revelry in the air, and the
white hail and the hoary flakes formed of snow and ice; and steam and fire,
the hideous lightning, and also the rainbow.

Spee uses homely language that is less individual than Traherne's, yet serves a similar purpose. To describe the sea as 'the drink', and suggest the howling of the wind by the common phrase 'Saus und Braus', is to bring poetry down from the pedestal on to which Hofmannswaldau, and sometimes Spee himself, had attempted to lift it.

Paul Fleming, on the other hand, whose formative years were spent outside Germany, on a long diplomatic journey through Russia and Persia, and who was influenced by the theosophical mysticism of Boehme, which placed him above the rivalry of sects, could compose a delicate love-poem in the Italian manner with some grace. In arguing with his coy mistress he was gentler than Hofmannswaldau or Marvell; he merely reminded her that time once passed never returns. Yet he too, although he called himself in writing his own epitaph 'Fortune's favourite son' ('des Glückes lieber Sohn'), was at his best in his poems of deep and unclouded religious feeling. At times he posed metaphysical questions, as in the first line of his sonnet 'Also hat Gott die Welt geliebet' ('God so loved the world'):

Ist's möglich, dasz der Hasz auch kann geliebet sein?[1]

to which he finds the answer:

Ja, Liebe, sonst war nichts, an dem du könntest weisen,
Wie stark dein Feuer sei, als an dem kalten Eisen
Der ausgestählten Welt.[2]

At other times as in his very well-known poem of acceptance, 'In allen meinen Taten' ('In all my deeds'), which Bach used as the text of his Cantata no. 97, he wrote in the four-square manner of the Lutheran hymn. Generally, however, he was more adventurous in his imagery than the supreme master of that form, Paul Gerhardt. He was, in fact, the most complete representative of the international Baroque style among the

[1] Is it possible that hatred also can be loved?
[2] Yes, beloved, or else there would be nothing by which you could show how strong your fire is except the cold iron of the steely world.

Germans. Yet, though he voiced the existential anxiety of
Chassignet, Gryphius, or Donne, he invariably concluded on a
note of triumphant acceptance. His sonnet to the Redeemer,
which begins with a cry for help:

Erhöre meine Not, du aller Not Erhörer![1]

ends in full reliance on Him who by His death redeemed the
world from death:

Arzt, ich bin krank nach dir. Du Brunnen Israel,
Dein kräftigs Wasser löscht den Durst der matten Seel.
Auch dein Blut, Osterlamm, hat meine Tür errötet,
Die zu dem Herzen geht. Ich steife mich auf dich,
Du mein Hort, du mein Fels. Belebe, Leben mich!
Dein Tod hat meinen Tod, du Todes Tod, getötet.[2]

Though Fleming's addiction to word-play and paradox is
at times rather too mechanical, he is capable, like Herbert, of
redeeming artificiality by the ecstatic strength of his feeling.
His puns spring rather from exuberant conviction than from
cold word-juggling. Ecstasy and elaborate word-play are the
hallmark also of the strange heretic Quirinus Kühlmann, who,
a generation later than Fleming, endeavoured to found his
own sect and ended his life at the stake in Moscow for preach-
ing his doctrine there. One of Kühlmann's inspirations for his
Kühlpsalmen or Cooling Psalms—the punning reference to
his own name is obvious—appears to have been a Latin
translation of the poetry of St John of the Cross.[3]
    Conflating three of the Spanish mystic's poems to make
his own 62nd Kühlpsalm, he transformed the comparatively
simple Renaissance verses into a Baroque *tour de force*. He did

[1] Hearken to my need, o hearkener to all needs!
[2] Doctor, I pine for you. O fount of Israel, your strong water quenches
the thirst of the weary soul. Your blood also, o Paschal Lamb, has reddened
my door, that leads to the heart. I prop myself on you, my shield, my rock.
Bring me to life, o life. Your death, o death of death, has slain my death.
[3] See Leonard Forster and A. A. Parker, 'Q.K. and the Poetry of St John
of the Cross', *Journal of Hispanic Studies*, vol. XXXV, no. 1 (Jan. 1958).

not, however, misrepresent the ideas or weaken the poetic tone of the original. He merely intensified St John's language, 'going for the vivid, colourful word, and pitching his voice high'.[1] Proceeding further, Kühlmann wrote a second part of the Psalm which was wholly original, and added a third which was not only original but incomprehensible. The second part, however, is as powerful as any German poetry of the period, and testifies to an idiosyncratic vision, which was perhaps more crazy than mystical. Kühlmann believed that every event in his life was symbolical and divinely ordered, and that he was destined to be the father of a new Messiah, as well as to found his new cult. Yet his poetry, like much of Christopher Smart's, which it somewhat resembles, has a power which transcends its craziness. Even if what was literal and symbolic truth to Kühlmann can be taken by the reader as no more than vivid metaphor, the second part of Psalm 62 will still retain its headlong cacophonous originality and its oblique references to the poems of St John which he had translated in the first part:

> Recht dunkelt mich das Dunkel,
> Weil Wesenheit so heimlichst anbeginnt!
> O seltner Glückskarfunkel!
> Es strömt, was aüszerlich verrinnt,
> Und wird ein Meer, was kaum ein Bächlein gründt.
> Je dunkler, je mehr lichter:
> Je schwärzer alls, je weiszer weiszt sein Sam.
> Ein himmlisch Aug ist Richter:
> Kein Irdscher lebt, der was vernahm;
> Es glänzt je mehr, je finster es ankam.[2]

Kühlmann was here using a shorter version of the *lira* measure, which Garcilaso had adopted from the Italian, and

[1] Forster and Parker, op. cit.

[2] It is right that darkness darkens for me, for thus essentiality most secretly begins. O rare carbuncle of fortune! What flows away outwardly now streams [inwardly], and what hardly fills a little brook becomes an ocean. The darker the lighter; the blacker everything is, the whiter his seed whitens. A heavenly eye is the judge: no mortal lives who has perceived anything of it. It gleams the more, the darker it approaches.

which had since become an habitual Spanish form. It had been used both by St John and his Latin translator. But though Kühlmann proved that it was admirably suited to his language, it was used by no other German poet, and Kühlmann himself abandoned it in other poems in favour of an exclamatory free verse which allowed him to indulge in his taste for catalogues of nouns and epithets that give many of his Psalms a certain hysterical power. In fact, however, they showed that language was no longer able to fulfil the tasks he set it.

Jakob Scheffler, too, some thirty years earlier, had reached the further limits of poetic utterance and withdrawn into an almost prosaic, though rhymed, simplicity. By birth a Protestant, and a doctor by profession, Scheffler adopted the title of Angelus Silesius ('the Silesian messenger') when he became a Catholic halfway through his career as a poet. His hymns in the Lutheran manner fall below the level of Paul Gerhardt's, though some of them survive in the hymn-books. He seems to woo God as the shepherdess woos her swain. Yet there is only a pretence of passion in his verse and none of the immediacy of language that is to be found in even the duller verses of Fleming and Spee. He uses the metaphors of the 'Song of Songs'. But in his hands, though spiritually valid, poetically it is dead. His rhymed apothegms couched in a manner that we associate today with cracker-mottoes are, however, both striking and authentic. These 'Geistliche Sinn- und Schluszreime' ('Apothegms and end-couplets') which he published with additions after his conversion, under the title of 'Der Cherubinische Wandersmann' ('The cherubic pilgrim'), are gnomic utterances which, though they seem to pass beyond the frontiers of poetry into some 'metapoetical' sphere, have at the same time the compression and the superimposed layers of meaning that one finds in poetry of the greatest kind.

> Die Seel, ein ewig Geist, ist über alle Zeit,
> Sie lebt auch in der Welt schon in der Ewigkeit.[1]

[1] The soul, an eternal spirit, exists out of all time. She lives even when in the world in eternity also.

In such lines as these the Silesian resolves the dichotomy in which his fellow-poets of the Baroque were so agonizingly caught. Eternity no longer speaks with the voice of thunder. It is the mysterious refuge in which the soul may dwell, even when still imprisoned in the net of time. The 'Cherubinische Wandersmann' not only passed beyond the frontiers of poetry but also beyond those of doctrinal particularism, into those provinces of the spirit where Eckhart, the Sufis, and the writers of the Upanishads speak with concordant voices:

> Ich selbst musz Sonne sein, ich musz mit meinen Strahlen
> Das farbenlose Meer der ganzen Gottheit malen.[1]

From these high spheres Scheffler was recalled to participate in the sordid sectarian disputes that rent his country. Having changed parties and afterwards taken holy orders as a Catholic priest, Scheffler added both to his hymns and his apothegms further books in which, however, theology clouded his vision, and later he unhappily stepped right down into the arena to publish his description of 'The Four Last Things', which contains a Struwwelpeter account, less compelling and less personal than Quevedo's, of the tortures of the damned. But his last additions to the 'Cherubinische Wandersmann' remain on a rare level. Indeed in his sixth and last book he wrote the epitaph of the whole Baroque age:

> Der Schiffer wirft im Sturm die schwersten Waren aus;
> Meinst du mit Gold beschwert zu komm'n ins Himmels
> Haus?[2]

The gold of style and metaphor ceased to be pursued in Germany after the seventies, a decade which saw the deaths of Gerhardt and Hofmannswaldau. They were survived by one or two of their followers and by the egregious Kühlmann, who

[1] I myself must be the sun, I must colour the colourless sea of the entire godhead with my beams.

[2] The sailor in a storm throws his heaviest cargo overboard. Do you expect to enter the heavenly mansion loaded with gold?

practised his own variant of the Baroque style in the next generation. Conditions were similar in other parts of Europe. Eclipsed in the sixties both in England and France, Baroque poetry survived after 1690 only among the lesser Marinists of Italy, and a few imitators of Góngora in Spain and her Empire, whose technical mannerisms hardened as their poetic originality diminished.

In music, alone among the arts, the Baroque convention survived into the next century. Indeed the greatest Baroque music was written when Classicism had mastered the poetry of every country. Throughout the Italian cantatas of Handel, for instance, the textual convention, to which the emotional colour of the music conforms, is completely Marinist. When Armida, abandoned by her lover, calls on the monsters of the deep to wreak vengeance on him, we are in the world of 'L'Adone'. It is the musical decoration, the equivalent in sound of the sensual descriptions which embellish and interrupt Marino's story, that holds the listener. The passions of the characters whom the singers pretend to impersonate are utterly unreal. When the Roman Agrippina, in another cantata by Handel, is condemned to death by her ungrateful son the Emperor Nero, she possesses no historical or poetic reality. She is merely a soprano voice rehearsing a number of moods. Nor does the monster Polyphemus of Handel's better-known English cantata 'Acis and Galatea' inspire even so much terror as Góngora's one-eyed Polifemo, who

> Un monte era de miembros eminente
> este que (de Neptuno hijo fiero)
> de un ojo ilustra el orbe de su frente,
> émulo casi del mayor lucero . . .[1]

Handel's Polyphemus represents the coarse voice of Nature more than half tamed by art. He is the clumsy villager who proclaims his rage and desire, and frightens the girls with his

---

[1] He was an outstanding mountain of human limbs, this cyclops, fierce son of Neptune. In his forehead, huge as an orb, shines a single eye, which could almost rival our greatest star, the sun. (Translation based on version by Dámaso Alonso.)

fee-fi-fo-fum threats. Yet really he is kind, comical, and pathetic by turns. The pastoral is here transformed into pantomime. Neither the blood nor the passions are to be taken seriously.

Johann Sebastian Bach, by contrast, inherited the Baroque concern with damnation, its morbid preoccupations with death, and its awareness of the flux of temporal life. Yet, unlike any poet of the seventeenth century except Milton, he was able to transform all these negative preoccupations into triumphant and positive emotion. This is true both of his Passions and his B minor Mass. But the process can be more conveniently examined in a work of smaller scale, his 62nd cantata, 'Ich will den Kreuzstab gerne tragen' ('I will gladly bear the cross'), which dwells on one of the major Baroque themes and uses familiar Baroque imagery. The text of the cantata was probably written by Bach himself. It was not, however, entirely original but was based on an earlier cantata text by a minor poet.

In the first recitative the bass compares his life to a sea voyage in which the waves daily threaten him with drowning; his only anchor is God's compassion, and the port for which he is bound is the Kingdom of Heaven. Though the cantata opens with a resolute acceptance of the Cross, the sense of abandonment and loss is strong in this recitative. The 'cello beneath the vocal line suggests the restless tossing of the waves, as the singer rises to declare the soul's sorrow, affliction, and distress ('Betrübnis, Kreuz, und Not'). The seas roar, and death makes its sombre entrance. Yet in the end all is well. The flux of life is transcended, the anchor of God's compassion holds on a sustained note, the voyager steps from the ship into his own city, and the journey is at an end:[1]

> So tret ich aus dem Schiff in meine Stadt,
> Die ist das Himmelreich,
> Wohin ich mit den Frommen
> Aus vieler Trübsal werde kommen.[2]

[1] See W. H. Whittaker, *Fugitive Notes on certain Cantatas and the Motets of J.S.B.*

[2] So I step from the ship into my city, which is the kingdom of heaven to which with the pious I shall come from great tribulation.

In his sorrow Bach has known the dereliction of the many poets who learnt in times of civil war that death was ever present and salvation hard to find. The texts of his cantatas dwell frequently on blood, tears, and hardship. Yet invariably all this vanishes in the confident joy of one who knows that his arrival at the long-desired port is certain. From the anguished mood of Sponde, Donne, or Gryphius, Bach comes to the candid confidence of Vaughan or Traherne. No Baroque artist expressed the emotion of joy so perfectly as Bach. All that he required was the single oboe with which he introduces and accompanies the aria 'Endlich, endlich wird mein Joch', or any one of a dozen others in the St Matthew Passion and the cantatas. Here, as in the far more elaborate 'Musical Offering' and in the Forty-nine Preludes and Fugues, he constructs the musical equivalents of those sonnets by Marino and Góngora in which ambiguities are stated, contrasted and reconciled, paradoxes are advanced and resolved, and the argument, adumbrated in the opening quatrain and developed in the second, is brought to a point in the first tercet and rounded off in the last. A technical exercise has been performed, and at the same time a work of art has been created.

Poetry, which at the beginning of the Baroque age had followed techniques akin to those of painting and sculpture, in the manner described by Heinrich Wölfflin, ended its course in close alliance with music, for which it provided text and libretto, and to which it finally left the expression of the deeper emotions which, by the close of the seventeenth century, it was powerless to interpret in its own medium. Born under the shadow of Michelangelo, it survived to be eclipsed by the genius of Johann Sebastian Bach.

Bibliography

English poetry

The Metaphysical Poets, selected and edited by Helen Gardner (Penguin Books, 1957; also O.U.P., 1961).

The Oxford Book of Seventeenth Century Verse, chosen by Sir Herbert Grierson and G. Bullough (O.U.P., 1934).

Also standard editions of Donne, Herbert, Crashaw, Milton, Vaughan and Traherne (O.U.P.) and Muses Library edition of Marvell (Routledge).

French poetry

The Penguin Book of French Verse, 2, introduced and edited by Geoffrey Brereton (Penguin Books, 1958).

Poètes du XVIème Siècle, texte établi et présenté par Albert-Marie Schmidt (Bibliothèque de la Pléiade, Gallimard, 1953). This book contains selections from du Bellay, Louise Labé, du Bartas, Desportes, Sponde, Chassignet, and several other poets.

Poésie du XVII ^ème Siècle, anthologie présenté par Thierry Maulnier (La Table Ronde, 1945).

Anthologie de la Poésie Baroque Française, texte choisie et présentée par Jean Rousset, 2 volumes (Editions de Cluny, 1961).

German poetry

Deutsche Gedichte des 16 and 17 Jahrhunderts, herausgegeben von Werner Milch (Verlag Lambert Schneider, Heidelberg, 1954).

Deutsche Dichtung des Barock, herausgegeben von Edgar Hederer (Carl Hanser Verlag, Munich, 1954 (?)).

The Penguin Book of German Verse, introduced and edited by Leonard Forster (Penguin Books, 1957). Though a general anthology, this book gives a very good selection from the Baroque poets.

Italian poetry

Marino e i Marinisti, a cura di Giuseppe Guido Ferrero (La Letteratura Italiana, storia e testi, volume 37 Ricciardi, 1954). This anthology gives an adequate selection from Marino, and from a number of the lesser Marinists.

Portuguese poetry

Luís de Camões, *Rimas*, texto establecido e prefaciado por Alvaro J. da Costa Pimpão (University of Coimbra 1953). Also standard editions of 'Os Lusíadas'.

Spanish poetry

José Manuel Blecua, Floresta lírica española (Editorial Gredos, Madrid, 1957). This is the best general anthology, and contains an interesting selection from the Baroque poets. There is no adequate seventeenth-century anthology, however. Standard editions of the chief poets vary greatly in the reliability of their texts. Selections from Góngora, Lope, and Quevedo, and a complete Garcilaso, appear in the cheap Ediciones Austral (Madrid and Buenos Aires).

The Penguin Book of Spanish Verse, introduced and edited by J. M. Cohen (Penguin Books, 1956).

Poetas novohispanos (1521–1621) and 2-volume (1621–1721) edición, selección y notas de Alfonso Méndez Plancarte (Imprenta Universitaria, México, 1942, 1943, and 1945). An excellent selection of poetry written in Mexico.

Criticism

The following books of criticism have contributed to the writing of this book, and treat a number of the ideas touched on in it:

Dámaso Alonso, *Poesía española*, Ensayo de métodos y limites estilísticos (Editorial Gredos, 1950). An interesting series of textual analyses of passages from the principal Spanish poets.

Dámaso Alonso, *Estudios y ensayos góngorinos* (Editorial Gredos, 1955). A collection of miscellaneous essays on Góngora and his contemporaries.

Dámaso Alonso, *Góngora y el 'Polifemo'*. An exhaustive analysis of a single poem, to which other material has been added in the second, 2-volume edition (1961).

Odette de Mourgues, *Metaphysical, Baroque and Précieux Poetry* (Oxford, 1953). An able comparison between the English and French poetry of the seventeenth century.

William Empson, *Seven Types of Ambiguity*, third edition (Chatto and Windus, 1953).

Oreste Macrí, *Fernando de Herrera* (Editorial Gredos, 1959). Translated from the Italian, this book not only presents a detailed study of the poet but a well-edited selection from his poetry, which includes many pieces not to be found in Vicente de Diego's revised *Clásicos castellanos* edition of 1952.

Emilio Orozco Díaz, *Temas del Barroco* (Universidad de Granada, 1947). A number of essays on such subjects as gardens and ruins, the Baroque poets' use of colour, the significance of the still-life, etc.

Emilio Orozco Díaz, *Introducción a un poema barroco granadino* (Universidad de Granada, 1955). Essays on the 'Soledades' of Góngora and on Pedro Soto de Rojos' 'Paraíso cerrado'.

J. Rousset, *La Littérature de l'Age Baroque en France* (Corti, 1953).

Die Kunstformen de Barockzeitalters, edited by Rudolf Stamm (Francke Verlag, Berne, 1956). A series of essays by various critics, which are of uneven value.

E. M. W. Tillyard, *The Metaphysicals and Milton* (Chatto and Windus, 1956).

Austin Warren, *Richard Crashaw* (Faber and Faber, 1957).

Heinrich Wölfflin, *Principles of Art History*, translated by M. D. Hottinger (Bell, 1926).

Index

This index includes, as well as those poets whose work is discussed in detail, a few important personalities of the time.

Achillini, Claudio, 46, 106, 140–1

Andrewes, Lancelot, 178

Angelus Silesius (Johann Scheffler), 195–6

Argensola, Bartolomé Leonardo de, 163–5, 166

Artale, Giuseppe, 119

Bach, Johann Sebastian, 152, 179, 189, 192, 198–9

Bocángel, Gabriel, 82–3, 103

Brives, Martial de, 160–1

Butler, Samuel, 146–7

Camões, Luís de, 18–19, 56–8, 130–1

Carew, Thomas, 116–17

Caro, Rodrigo, 24–5, 49

Castiglione, Baldassare, 52, 58–9

Chassignet, Jean - Baptiste, 41–3, 50

Claude le Lorrain, 97

Colonna, Vittoria, 59

Crashaw, Richard, 105–6, 154–5

Cruz, Sor Juana Inés de la, 83–6

De la Tour, Georges, 41

Desportes, Philippe, 62–3

Donne, John, 44–5, 58–9, 112–13, 125–8, 166–9, 170–1

Du Bartas, Guillaume, 110–12

Du Bellay, Joachim, 17–18, 23–4, 37, 40, 89

Du Bois Hus, 158–9

Espinosa, Pedro, 81–2

Fleming, Paul, 192–3

Fontanella, Girolamo, 113–15, 153–4

Garcilaso de la Vega, 34–6

Gerhardt, Paul, 189–90

Giovanetti, Marcello, 67

Godeau, A., 160–1

Góngora, Luis de, 71–9, 80–1, 87, 120–3, 134–8, 197

Gryphius, Andreas, 20–1, 43–4, 169–70

Guevara, Fray Miguel de, 165

Handel, George Frederick, 197–8

Herbert, George, 173–6, 177–80

Herrera, Fernando de, 19, 36, 55–6, 131–3

Hobbema, Meindert, 100, 106

Hofmann von Hofmannswaldau, Christian, 49–50, 88

Jáuregui, Juan de, 80–1

Kühlmann, Quirinus, 193–4

La Ceppède, Jean de, 155–8, 169, 171–3

Labé, Louise, 60–1

Lubrano, Giacomo, s. J., 115–16

Malherbe, François de, 138–40, 144–5, 159–60

Marino, Giambattista, 25–9, 46, 63–5, 70, 104–5, 106–7, 154–5, 167–8

Marvell, Andrew, 22, 87, 88, 89–91, 92–3, 98–100, 135, 142–4

Michelangelo Buonarotti, 33–4, 52–5

Milton, John, 107–8, 151–2, 153, 159

Monteverdi, Claudio, 105, 120

Morando, Conte Bernardo, 67–8, 70

Paoli, Pier Francesco, 47

Pascal, Blaise, 16, 79

Pers, Ciro di, 46–7, 102–3

Poussin, Nicholas, 100

Quevedo, Francisco de, 21–3, 26–9, 47–9, 117–18, 123–5, 145

Racine, Jean, 162

Raphael, 32

Rembrandt, 11, 32–3

Ronsard, Pierre de, 16–17, 38–9, 61–2

Rosa, Salvator, 80

Rubens, P. P., 100, 106

Ruysdael, Jakob, 100, 106

Saint-Amant, Marc-Antoine de, 95, 96–7, 100–1, 118–19

Sandoval y Zapata, Luis de, 86–7

Sarbiewski, Maciej Kazi-
    mierz, 65–6
Shakespeare, William, 34,
    52–4
Shirley, James, 148–9
Soto de Rojas, Pedro, 91–2,
    93–5, 99
Spee, Friedrich von, 190–2
Sponde, Jean de, 19–20, 38–42
Stampa, Gaspara, 59–60

Traherne, Thomas, 185–9
Tristan L'Hermite, 66–7, 147

Vaughan, Henry, 180–5
Vega, Lope de, 162–3
Velázquez, Diego, 76, 119–20
Viau, Théophile de, 40, 97–8

Zurbarán, Francisco, 109–10